# breastfeeding
## *...naturally*

### second edition

Edited by Jill Day

australian
breastfeeding
association

National Library of Australia
Cataloguing-in-Publication data:

Breastfeeding ...naturally.

2nd ed.
Includes index.
ISBN 1 921001 02 X

1. Breast feeding. 2. Motherhood. I. Day, Jill. II. Australian Breastfeeding Association. III. Title.


649.33


Edited by Jill Day
for the Australian Breastfeeding Association

First published 1996 (edited by Jane Cafarella)
Second edition 2004
Minor revision 2006

Published and distributed by
AUSTRALIAN BREASTFEEDING ASSOCIATION
(formerly Nursing Mothers' Association of Australia)
1818–1822 Malvern Road, East Malvern VIC 3145


Printed in Australia by Ligare Pty Ltd, Riverwood NSW


*Cover photographs by:*
*Susan D'Arcy, Vicki Bell, Daina Booth, Dez Murad, Karen Powell and Trish Sharkey*

# breastfeeding

## ...naturally

second edition

# CONTENTS

australian
breastfeeding
association

# FOREWORD

*Wendy Burge*

*How refreshing to find a book jam-packed with all the no-nonsense tips and information that everyone has come to expect from the Australian Breastfeeding Association (formerly Nursing Mothers).*

The easy-reading style and practical suggestions found in the association's extensive range of highly-regarded booklets have been re-created here in one easily-dipped-into volume.

The Australian Breastfeeding Association was proud to publish *Breastfeeding ...naturally* in 1996, in answer to the community's need for the most up-to-date information about breastfeeding and breastmilk. As more and more research focuses on the marvels of breastfeeding, subtle shifts in understandings, requirements and recommendations mean that the association is constantly revising its printed literature, and the way we work with families and the community.

Despite the fast-changing pace of life, family structures and society's expectations, breastmilk continues to offer the nutrition nature meant for our babies. Breastfeeding is an irreplaceable experience for both baby and mother and an excellent foundation for a deeply nurturing relationship between them. From its work with many thousands of families, the Australian Breastfeeding Association understands that up-to-date information and quality support at the crucial times are fundamental to getting the best out of breastfeeding.

It is exciting and fitting to launch this revised edition of *Breastfeeding ...naturally* during the association's 40th birthday year. It is a timely reminder of the value of continuing to strive for increased understanding and practical knowledge. I trust *Breastfeeding ...naturally* will continue to inspire mothers and their families to maintain that precious breastfeeding bond and to actively see the worth in providing our children with nature's intended first food — breastmilk.

Please enjoy *Breastfeeding ...naturally*, and enjoy breastfeeding your baby.

*Wendy Burge*
*President 2004, Australian Breastfeeding Association*

CHAPTER ONE

# A commitment to breastfeeding

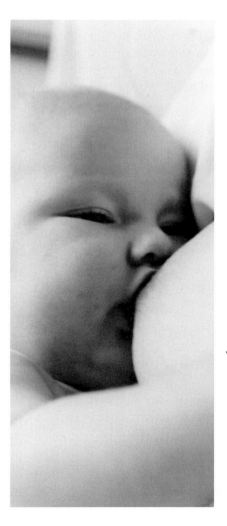

Photograph by Susan D'Arcy

- Why breastfeeding is important
- Breastfeeding is a healthy investment for both babies and mothers
- Protecting the environment
- The pleasures of breastfeeding
- Be part of the breastfeeding sisterhood

*Breastfeeding gives me a sense of fulfilment beyond compare. It was something only I can do for my baby.*

Photograph by Davina Hurst

Congratulations on your commitment to breastfeed your baby. You are ensuring that your baby has the best possible start in life and that you are getting the most out of motherhood.

Your commitment may have been based on watching and listening to other breastfeeding mothers, or on information you have picked up in other books or in the media, or perhaps it simply feels right for you and your baby. Whatever your motivation, you can feel confident that your instincts are right. Breastmilk is the optimum food for your baby and a convenient and pleasurable choice for you.

Perhaps the best answer if someone asks you whether you intend to breastfeed is: 'Naturally!'

*The 2001 National Health Survey showed that 87 percent of infants aged between 0–3 years had, at some stage, obtained nutrition from breastmilk — a similar figure to 1995 (86 percent).*

*Australian Bureau of Statistics, publication 4810.0.55.001, Breastfeeding in Australia, September 2003*

## What's in it for babies?

Reminding yourself just how important breastfeeding is will give you confidence in your commitment. Human milk is a complex mix of ingredients that not only nourish and protect your baby, but also help to regulate his growth and his metabolism in a host of subtle ways. And the incredible closeness between you and your breastfed baby provides a sense of bonding that can never be overstated. It's a closeness that will be with you forever.

### The perfect match

Not only is your breastmilk a constantly-adapting living fluid, changing to meet your baby's developing needs, it is also a perfect (and unique) match with your baby. No two mothers' milk is exactly the same. Your breastmilk contains antibodies to help protect your baby from the illnesses you are both exposed to, and the mix of anti-infective properties and nutrients adapts from feed to feed.

## A balanced meal

Breastmilk provides complete, balanced meals for your baby for his first six months. It is there wherever and whenever he needs them, and it continues to be the most important part of his diet throughout his first year. It satisfies both his hunger and his thirst.

Breastmilk has just the right amount of protein, fats, salts, sugars and other nutrients. Your baby easily utilises the calcium in breastmilk, and the iron absorbed through breastmilk is sufficient to maintain normal reserves for at least six months. The small, soft curds of breastmilk are perfect for your baby's sensitive digestive system.

## Food to stay or go

Whether your baby prefers a quiet night at home or the fresh air and stimulation at his favourite lunch spot in the park, he can be assured that his favourite food will always be available. It's always at just the right temperature, and it's jam-packed with all the nutrition your baby needs.

## Ongoing protection

When your baby is born, his immune system is relatively undeveloped — this development happens over the first 9 to 12 months. Breastfeeding protects your baby during this time, and without it, he is vulnerable to illness and infection.

The colostrum your new baby receives in the first few days provides special protection as he makes the transition from the safety of the womb to his new world. The anti-infective properties of breastmilk are maintained for as long as breastfeeding continues, whether this is weeks, months or years. Breastfeeding provides protection against bowel and respiratory illnesses and can also protect against urinary tract infections well after weaning.

Ensuring your baby has only breastmilk for at least six months will help minimise allergy problems.

Fully-breastfed infants are rarely constipated and have a low incidence of gastrointestinal illnesses. Babies who don't receive breastmilk, on the other hand, have a significantly greater risk of contracting gastroenteritis and are more likely to become constipated.

Illnesses such as middle ear infections and eczema that have come

*Breastfeeding gives me a sense of fulfilment beyond compare. It was something only I can do for my baby. I am so proud of myself for what we have achieved. I stroke her hair and pat her softly and talk to her as she nestles her face against my breast.*

to be regarded as part of the normal trials of childhood are much more common in babies who don't receive breastmilk.

There is no risk of contamination. Breastmilk is delivered straight from breast to baby, and there are no storage problems.

Your breastfed baby's nutritional needs will not be threatened by blackouts, natural disasters or emergencies.

## A healthy investment

Breastfeeding your baby is an investment in his future health, an investment that will not only benefit him as an individual and you as a family, but the community in general. His resistance to infection will mean fewer doctor and hospital visits. In fact, breastmilk can be viewed as a source of preventative medicine in addition to being a source of nutrition.

Research shows that breastfed babies have the best chance of reaching their full IQ potential. This is thought to be partly because breastmilk contains the fatty acids important for brain development in addition to other components still to be identified. Recently, new components found in human milk have been added to some infant formulas. However, the complexity of these components and the way in which they change with the needs of individual babies can't be copied. Just adding some of them to formula doesn't mean that they will act in the same way as they do in breastmilk.

The action of breastfeeding enhances eyesight, speech and jaw development.

Tooth decay is rare in breastfed infants and breastfeeding guards against obesity in later life.

Breastfeeding is linked with a lower risk of sudden infant death syndrome (SIDS).

Children who have been infant-formula-fed have a higher incidence of diseases such as juvenile diabetes, childhood cancers such as leukaemia, and coeliac disease.

*Why do I breastfeed? I breastfeed because it is how human females were designed to nurture their young. I breastfeed because it allows me precious close time with my daughter. I breastfeed because it ensures my daughter is getting optimum nutrition, antibodies, and will have smaller chances of contracting major diseases. I breastfeed because it is convenient, portable and easy and because she can have access to it anytime she wants. If I wanted to go out without her I could express enough milk for her to drink. I breastfeed because it eases her discomforts, it nurtures her soul as well as her body, and it offers a warm, safe and peaceful place to be when she is sad or hurts herself.*

## It's a pleasure

Cuddling is a natural by-product of breastfeeding. Your baby will enjoy the warmth and security of being close to you. He can feel the warmth and softness of your skin and hear your heartbeat.

Breastfeeding is not just a feeding relationship; it's a nurturing relationship. Touch is a fundamental human need. Skin-to-skin contact during breastfeeding promotes a sense of wellbeing in your baby (and in you).

## What's in it for you?

There is a common misconception that women breastfeed just because it's good for their babies, rather than because it's good for them. But the truth is that breastfeeding is not a selfless act. Once you have established a good breastfeeding relationship with your baby, being a mother is just so much easier.

*Photograph by Dez Murad*

### A healthy investment for you too

Just as breastfeeding has long-term health benefits for babies, it is important for mothers too. Ongoing research shows that if mothers don't breastfeed, they increase their risks of osteoporosis and cancer of the breast and ovaries.

### A better night's sleep

Consider this: it's 2 am and your new baby is crying for a feed. You can nudge your partner to bring your baby to you, roll on your side, put your baby to your breast while cradling him with your arm, and drift gently back to sleep, aided by the release of relaxing hormones triggered by the baby's sucking. (Note safe bed-sharing guidelines; see page 109.)

Or you can put on your dressing gown and slippers, turn on the kitchen light, remove the bottle of infant formula — which you made up earlier that evening after disinfecting the bottle, teat and other equipment — and boil some water to heat it up. (You can't use the microwave as it may heat unevenly and burn your baby's mouth.) You

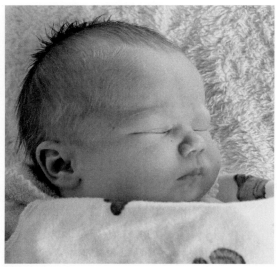

*Photograph by Lou Slater*

can then return to your now screaming baby and sit up in a chair or your bed while feeding.

When the baby has finished and perhaps drifted off to sleep, you can then put him back in his bed and return to your own.

In these circumstances, which in the early months may occur several times a night, which would you prefer — breastfeeding or bottle-feeding? More importantly, which would your baby prefer?

## Life is simple

If you are bottle-feeding, the need to carry infant formula, disinfected bottles, teats and water for mixing everywhere you go makes going out a chore, and there's always the worry that you'll either run out of formula or that it will go off in the heat.

Artificial feeding also means your baby is vulnerable during emergencies where access to clean water, methods of boiling water, and heating and refrigeration are limited.

If you have your breastfed baby with you, being held up while waiting at the doctor's, or for the train or just being faced with a hungry baby while you are in a department store are all situations that are easily dealt with.

A breastfeeding mother can also return to paid work whenever she is ready. Continuing to breastfeed may also help alleviate feelings of separation and the guilt that, regrettably but inevitably, seem to haunt mothers in paid work. You can be reassured that you are still providing the best food for your baby, even if you can't always be there.

## You save money

Breastfeeding costs nothing apart from a small increase in your food intake.

Bottle-feeding, by comparison, is expensive — not only in the purchase of the infant formula, but in the resources needed to produce, package and deliver it. Another cost factor rarely taken into account is the medical backup required when a baby becomes ill through lower resistance to infection or due to contamination of formula.

A bottle-fed baby is also more vulnerable if money is short and the family struggles to find enough money to buy formula — something that aid agencies in Australia report is quite common, particularly where parents depend on pensions or benefits.

## It gets you back in shape

Breastfeeding aids the contraction of your uterus, helping it return to its pre-pregnant state as nature designed. A formula-feeding mother will usually take longer to return to her pre-pregnancy figure.

## Delayed menstruation

Your periods usually don't return for many months if you breastfeed your baby exclusively (where your baby receives only breastmilk). This is more convenient for you, it saves money, and reduces the impact of tampons and sanitary napkins on the environment.

## Nature's contraceptive

A breastfeeding mother is generally infertile — if she is breastfeeding exclusively, her baby is less than six months, and she has not recommenced her menstrual cycle.

## Sweet as a rose

Many new mothers are quite surprised at how sweet their breastfed babies smell. Their baby's breath is sweet and even his stools are comparatively sweet smelling. This is another natural benefit of breastfeeding. Babies can be messy creatures: what goes in eventually comes out, sometimes at both ends — hopefully not simultaneously. Breastfeeding helps makes the task of cleaning them up less odorous as well as less arduous.

## No qualifications required

A mother does not have to be literate to breastfeed, and human error cannot affect the composition of breastmilk. Where literacy rates are low, the bottle-fed baby's survival can depend on a parent's ability to read and follow instructions for making up infant formula.

> *Knowing that my baby was growing and healthy, and that he had achieved that — we had achieved that together — with my breastmilk alone, was the most amazing feeling I have ever had.*

## Empowerment

Knowing that you alone are able to provide all the nutrition that your baby needs for the first six months of life can be empowering and uplifting. Breastfeeding can be very liberating and make you feel confident and powerful as a woman.

## It's a pleasure for Mum too

Breastfeeding your baby is relaxing and pleasurable and helps you make the most of motherhood. The release of relaxing hormones as you feed helps you to bond with your child and to feel good. It gives you lots of opportunities for you to sit down, put your feet up and enjoy your baby. Breastfeeding gives you both a special feeling of closeness and is intensely fulfilling emotionally.

As your baby grows, he will use this time to get to know you, gazing into your eyes, stroking your breast fondly, maybe playing with your hair and clothing. It is these moments of joy that make the hard work of mothering worthwhile.

In short, for an independent woman, breastfeeding offers maximum independence and makes mothering a pleasure.

# Baby greenies

Breastmilk is possibly the 'greenest' food your child will ever have. It is produced at little cost to the physical environment. What's good for babies is also good for the environment.

Gabrielle Palmer in her book *The Politics of Breastfeeding* talks about the economic value of human milk — something that is rarely, if ever, stated. She says: 'Human milk is a commodity which is ignored in national inventories and disregarded in food consumption surveys, yet it does actually save a country millions of dollars in imports and health costs.'

Infant-formula-feeding uses energy and resources. Forests are depleted to provide fuel; tin is mined and later discarded; physical and intellectual resources are used to manufacture formula; large tracts of land are needed to breed animals to provide the milk; fertiliser, used to maintain the land, pollutes our waters.

Breastfeeding not only saves lives, it saves energy, natural resources and money not just for a baby's family but for the whole nation.

> The health costs of weaning 30 percent of infants on to infant formula by three months of age could be around $20 million a year in Australia. This is based on an analysis of just five illnesses for which breastfeeding is proved to have protective effects. The total value of breastfeeding to the community makes it one of the most cost-effective primary prevention measures available and well worth the support of the entire community.
>
> Food for Health: Dietary Guidelines for Children and Adolescents in Australia, Commonwealth Department of Health and Ageing and NHMRC, 2003

## The breastfeeding sisterhood

Having your own child suddenly changes your perspective, both domestically and globally. Images in the media of suffering mothers and children may suddenly be extremely disturbing to you, as you now identify more strongly with them.

As such, you may consider your decision to breastfeed to be a political statement, as well as something that is right and natural for you and your baby.

Advances in science and stricter controls on the composition and advertising of infant formula, as well as better hygiene, have lessened, but not eliminated, the dangers of bottle-feeding in the developed world. In many parts of the world, particularly where resources such as water and energy are limited, and where many women are illiterate, the difference between breastfeeding and bottle-feeding often means the difference between life and death.

Despite the 1981 World Health Organization International Code of Marketing of Breast-milk Substitutes (known as the WHO Code), babies are still dying in both the developed and the developing world as a consequence of the promotion of these products.

*Photograph by Susan D'Arcy*

The implementation of the WHO Code in Australia is confined to a narrow, voluntary and unenforceable manufacturers' agreement covering marketing of infant formula. Strong government support for breastfeeding really does make a difference in breastfeeding rates. In Scandinavian countries, where there is a strong breastfeeding culture as well as adherence to the WHO Code, breastfeeding rates are the highest in the world. In the United Kingdom, where there is little support for breastfeeding mothers and where most of the information about infant feeding comes from formula companies, only one in five babies is receiving breastmilk at six months.

Your commitment to breastfeed your own child shows solidarity with mothers who are struggling to do so all over the world against great odds. And by not purchasing infant formula yourself you are not endorsing its promotion here or in the developing world.

CHAPTER TWO

# The concept of choice

Photograph by Simone Hanckel

*There is a common misconception, even today, that the only difference between bottle-feeding and breastfeeding is the container.*

- *The choices are not equal*
- *The issue of guilt*
- *The influence of our culture*
- *Common concerns of mothers in making decisions about infant feeding*
- *Family views and how things have changed*

*Photograph by Simone Hanckel*

People usually talk about mothers choosing to breastfeed, but the reality is that breastfeeding actually chooses you. Breastfeeding is an integral part of the reproductive continuum — the final stage of the conception-pregnancy-birth cycle. Your body is programmed by nature to produce breastmilk for your new baby. As with other aspects of the cycle, you can actively choose to turn it off. However, when a woman chooses not to breastfeed, it's important that she does so with a full understanding of the consequences for herself and for her baby. Babies must live with the consequences, both in the short and long term, even though they have no say in the 'choice'.

## Some choices aren't equal

There is a common misconception, even today, that the only difference between bottle-feeding and breastfeeding is the container — one comes in a breast and one comes in a bottle, and while the breast may be conveniently attached, the bottle is even more conveniently detached so that others can feed the baby too. Even if this were true, there is no doubt that babies would prefer the nice warm, soft breast to silicone and a hard bottle.

But the truth is that in comparing infant formula with breastmilk, you are not comparing equals. While science may have made some improvements to infant formulas and modern hygiene makes their delivery less risky, there is no formula that comes close to the life-giving and life-saving properties of breastmilk, a fact that the infant formula companies cannot dispute.

For most women, electing to feed their babies artificially is a compromise rather than a choice — a compromise that is often the result of conflicting and inaccurate advice and lack of support. All mothers deserve not only the right technical advice and support to breastfeed; they need the confidence and determination to stand up for their rights and for the rights of their baby.

Wanting to breastfed your child is not about demanding something special and different. It's simply what mothers do. It's a fundamental human right.

# The guilt trip

Sadly, when this right is not recognised, it is often seen as a failure on the part of the mother, rather than of society and the medical system. This leads to a circle of blame and guilt that divides mothers. In a culture where women are still largely socialised to accept responsibility — even for things over which they have no control — it is not surprising that they blame themselves, and each other, when things go wrong.

The vast majority of bottle-feeding mothers in Australia found themselves in a situation where they felt that there was no choice left, that breastfeeding had proved too difficult. Guilt is the wrong word here. Perhaps 'regret' is a more appropriate term — regret that no-one around them could help them fix the problem.

# Fighting cultural perceptions

Breastfeeding may be the natural and normal way to feed a baby, but whether it is culturally promoted is open to question.

The symbol of the feeding bottle to represent a baby is as pervasive in our culture as the golden arches. The symbol of the breast is also pervasive. Despite moves to wipe out sexist advertising, the breast is still used both overtly and covertly to advertise everything from jeans to holidays.

In Western culture the breast is an erotic symbol rather than a symbol of nurture. This can create quite a mental hurdle for some women who are considering breastfeeding, or trying to breastfeed. To feed your baby in a crowded cafe, for example, you may have to overcome your own embarrassment and that of other people around you who may only see breasts in their erotic role.

In a 2001 Australian Breastfeeding Association study of women's experiences of breastfeeding, the thing they wanted most was a society in which the importance of breastfeeding was universally acknowledged and in which there was wider community understanding of how breastfeeding *really* works.

There is still a great deal of ignorance about how breastfeeding works. Many people, including health professionals, take on board — and sadly pass on — information that is incorrect, contradictory or inconsistent.

Some of this conflicting information is the result of very limited education on lactation, lack of access to new research and an unwillingness to accept new information. It takes a long time to change accepted medical attitudes and practices. One example of this is the length of a breastfeed. Twenty to thirty years ago, women were encouraged to begin breastfeeding slowly, feeding one minute on each breast per feed on the first day, three minutes on the second day, five minutes on the third day, gradually building up to ten minutes on each side for each feed. It was thought that this would help prevent sore nipples. However, later research has shown that this is not the case, that good positioning and attachment are important in preventing sore nipples and that longer feeds in the early days help stimulate milk supply and prevent engorgement. Yet, even today, many mothers are advised to limit feeds, showing just how long it can take for basic information to become accepted practice.

While most mothers assume that all health professionals know all there is to know about breastfeeding, the reality is that lactation receives little attention in training programs. What education and information they do receive is often provided by infant formula companies, whose focus is unsurprisingly on increasing sales of their product. With advertising direct to mothers now limited, most advertising of infant formula is directed to health professionals. It is therefore encouraging to see that some health professionals, who recognise that they have a responsibility to provide informed and unbiased advice, actively seek out accurate and ethical lactation education programs and resources.

## Why would anyone choose to feed artificially?

Why, despite the many benefits of breastfeeding, and the many risks associated with bottle-feeding, even with modern-day hygiene, do some women choose to bottle-feed?

One reason may be how information of infant feeding is presented. Sometimes, in a misguided effort to avoid making mothers who choose artificial feeding feel guilty, it is presented as an equal choice.

Author and lactation expert Diane Wiessinger, wrote in the *Journal of Human Lactation* about an infant feeding 'preference card' that was presented to new mothers at a United States maternity centre. It listed odourless stools and a return of the uterus to its normal size among five breastfeeding advantages. Disadvantages included leaking breasts and the inability to see how much the baby was getting. An advantage of artificial feeding was said to be that some mothers found it less inhibiting and embarrassing.

This may sound reasonable until you present other health issues in the same way. Wiessinger uses information about smoking as an example. 'One disadvantage of not smoking is that you are more likely to find second-hand smoke annoying. One advantage of smoking is that it can contribute to weight loss,' she writes. It is easy to see how this so-called 'balanced' approach masks the considerable health risks of smoking. As Wiessinger says: 'The real issue is differential morbidity and mortality. In other words, smokers are less healthy and have higher death rates.'

The same can be said for so-called balanced information about artificial feeding. The reality is that according to the World Health Organization, artificial feeding does not even rank second-best when compared to breastfeeding. It lists the following hierarchy: 1) breastfeeding; 2) the mother's own milk expressed and given to her child some other way; 3) the milk of another human mother; and 4) artificial milk feeds.

While you might feel sure that the following common concerns will not impact on your own decisions about breastfeeding, they are worth examining now. Some time down the track, they may become factors in whether or not you continue to breastfeed.

### 'I want my own space'

Our ideas about mothering (and breastfeeding) are coloured by the values society places on that role and on the other roles we are expected to play. In a society where the needs of the individual are most important, and in which parenting comes to us later and later in life, it's hardly surprising that the thought of having someone totally dependent on us can seem pretty scary.

The fact that, for the most part, only paid work is seen as real work hides the demands of parenting from many young people. Parenting, particularly mothering, where much more physical intimacy is involved, is extremely hard work. Most parents look back with a wry smile when they recall telling everyone that this baby was just going to 'fit in' to their life.

Real babies may be cute and cuddly, with skin as soft as an angel's wings, but their needs are far from tiny. Babies are human beings with human needs — none of which they are capable of meeting themselves. Like you, they get hungry between meals, they get uncomfortable, and they get sick,

> *While awaiting the birth of my first baby, I tried to envisage what life would be like after he/she was born, and considered doing a course of study as I thought the baby would sleep for a minimum of four hours between feeds. How else would I fill in all that time, I wondered? Little did I know!*

tired, itchy, grumpy and bored. The difference is that they can only cry about it, while you can talk about it and actually do something about it.

Breastfeeding allows you space to put aside less important things while you and your baby enjoy each other. The vital nutrients your baby gets from your milk, and the skin-to-skin contact are far more valuable than a tidy house, both in the short and long term.

### 'My partner might feel left out'

Photograph by Susan D'Arcy

Sometimes, women are discouraged by their partners from breastfeeding because they fear that they may be excluded from bonding with their baby or because they are envious of the physical and emotional closeness between mother and child.

The birth of a new baby is an emotional time for everyone, especially if this is your first child, and it takes time to adjust from being a couple to a family.

In the past, stereotypical notions of how men and women should behave meant that fathers were excluded from most aspects of child care, not just feeding. Today however, most fathers are enthusiastic partners in the preparation, the birth itself and the care of their child.

It is important from the start not to allow parenting to turn into a competition for your baby's affection. Your partner needs to be reassured that while feeding is vital for your baby's survival, cuddling, playing and loving are important too. He can still enjoy bonding with his baby and skin-to-skin contact through carrying, bathing and baby massage. And he may sometimes feed his baby expressed breastmilk when you can't be there.

Talk to your partner about why you want to breastfeed, and share your feelings with each other. Encourage him to read this book and to talk to other fathers whose partners have breastfed.

All fathers, as well as mothers, want the best for their babies, and breastmilk is indisputably the best food a baby can have. Reassure your partner that the best thing he can do for his baby is to support your commitment to breastfeed. He may be surprised at the rewards he receives, too. Fathers often say that seeing their baby breastfeeding is an intensely emotional and rewarding experience.

*'Just the thought of breastfeeding turns me off'*

Negative feelings about our body's natural functions sometimes lead to a confusion of feelings about breastfeeding. Some people view breastmilk as waste matter that is eliminated from the body. Breastmilk is not an excretion, but a secretion. It is not related to waste products such as urine or sweat but is 'a living fluid', different from, but more closely related to blood. Just as blood contains living substances which give our body energy, breastmilk carries nutrients from mother to baby.

Cows' milk is also a secretion. However, the same people who are revolted by the idea of breastmilk, find the idea of quaffing huge quantities of cows' milk udderly delightful! Perhaps if breastmilk was packaged differently, in cardboard cartons with pictures of sports people on them, or if cows' milk was drunk straight from the udder, the correlation would be more obvious.

If it is not the milk, but the very notion of somebody feeding from your breasts that is distasteful, then it can help to talk to other women about what breastfeeding actually feels like, particularly those who may have felt uncomfortable about it at first. Some women who may have been 'turned off' at the idea but who tried it anyway, have been surprised to find it's not at all unpleasant. In fact most women find it very pleasurable indeed.

Pregnancy and birth bring many physical and emotional changes. In a society that reveres the body shape of the immature woman, slim and taut, it is very confronting for a woman to find her body ripening and expanding. She may feel very vulnerable, but she may also feel very powerful. In every way, breastfeeding is a feminist statement. It is a tremendous and amazing thing to be able to produce another human being from your own body and then to be able to nurture that being solely from your own body for the first six months. It is a great achievement, and many women, including those with brilliant careers, see it as their greatest achievement. Viewed like this, breastfeeding can help you feel more positive about your body and about being a woman.

*'Breastfeeding will ruin my figure'*

Comments like 'You'll have boobs down to your waist!' are annoyingly common when you're breastfeeding, especially if you continue to feed your baby past early infancy. Not only is this a fallacy, the facts point as firmly as a bullet bra in the other direction.

Breastfeeding is unjustly blamed for the figure changes that occur during pregnancy; but studies have shown little ultimate difference between the bodies of mothers who have breastfed and those who have bottle-fed. The reality is that motherhood brings a maturing of the female body. Unless you have the discipline and the money to train your body close to its previous taut youthful state, you may have to accept the new you. This is not an excuse to let yourself go. Moderate exercise will help you look and feel better; but in the final analysis, you will probably look and feel a little different after giving birth — and this is natural. Your new role may mean a loss of your youthful shape, but it will also bring many more gains as you mature and grow as a mother.

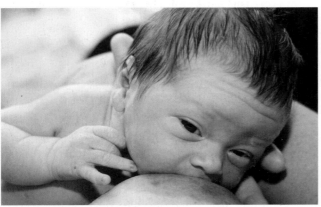

*Photograph by Helen Tidy*

### 'Breastfeeding will hurt'

Breastfeeding should not hurt providing a baby is attached properly and sucking well. In fact, for most mothers it is a pleasurable experience. While some nipple and breast soreness can occur in the early stages, with the right information, support and treatment, this can be easily and quickly solved.

Breastfeeding is not about a mother suffering for the good of her child. If she is experiencing pain, there is something wrong and it should be attended to immediately.

It is impossible to nurture your child if you are doing it through gritted teeth and indeed, persevering through pain defeats one of the benefits of breastfeeding, which is to build a positive, nurturing relationship with your baby.

### 'I want to eat whatever I like'

Despite the commercially-driven notion that breastfeeding women need to have a special diet or dietary supplements, you don't have to eat or drink any particular foods or follow anything other than your normal diet in order to breastfeed successfully. You may just find you are thirstier and hungrier than usual in the early days.

Breastfeeding is designed so that your baby gets top priority when the nutrients are handed out, no matter what you eat. Your body will still produce nourishing milk for your baby even if you are undernourished. You can live on cola and French fries and still breastfeed successfully. However, you are obviously going to feel better (and look better) if you are eating a normal healthy diet.

### 'Mum bottle-fed me, and I'm healthy'

When you become a mother, you often begin to understand your own mother more, and to want to be close to her, both geographically and emotionally. You may find that she enjoys helping you care for your baby and this may also mean encouraging you to do as she did.

If your mother breastfed, this will be an invaluable support; but if she did not, you may find that your decision to breastfeed puts you at odds with her own choices about infant feeding. She may be unable to support you simply because she is not really sure how breastfeeding works.

Having raised her own children successfully on infant formula she may be unable to see any obvious differences between bottle-fed babies and breastfed babies. Although you won't want to criticise your own mother's mothering techniques or to jeopardise your relationship, your decision to breastfeed your baby should not be based on whether your mother breastfed her children 20 or more years ago, but on

*Photograph by Susan D'Arcy*

what is right for you and your baby today. Like you, your mother would have based her care and feeding of you on the best knowledge and support that was available to her. By choosing to feed your baby naturally, you are not going against family tradition or undermining your mother.

In the early 1970s, breastfeeding rates in Australia were at their lowest. Women born at this time are now having babies and their own mothers are unable to help them, as they haven't experienced breastfeeding. If a mother sees her daughter or daughter-in-law struggling or in pain, what advice does she offer? 'You were on the bottle, and you turned out alright.' This is the time to talk to someone experienced in successful breastfeeding, not women who weaned because they got bad advice.

Your immediate family or other relatives may think that your baby's dependence on you for food means they will be excluded from her care or involvement in her life. Fortunately, this isn't true. There are many things they can do to bond with the baby, apart from feed it. They may not be able to prepare a feed for the baby in the early days, but feeding the rest of the family will no doubt be a welcome offer.

By supporting you in your commitment to breastfeeding, they are part of ensuring your baby only has the best.

*When the Australian Breastfeeding Association first started in 1964 (known then as the Nursing Mothers' Association), only 23 percent of mothers were breastfeeding on discharge from hospital. By comparison, the 2001 National Health Survey showed that 83 percent of all Australian 0–3-year-olds were breastfed on discharge from hospital.*

*2001 figures supplied by the Australian Bureau of Statistics, publication 4810.0.55.001 Breastfeeding in Australia, September 2003.*

CHAPTER THREE

# How breastfeeding works

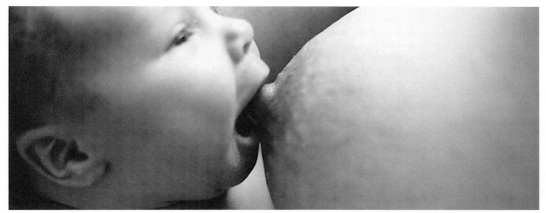

*Photograph by Susan D'Arcy*

*When my brain made sense of breastfeeding, it seemed that my breasts and I did too!*

- The changes that occur to breasts during pregnancy and after birth

- Anatomy of the breast

- How the breast makes milk

- The let-down reflex and the principle of supply and demand

- How breastmilk changes to suit the baby

- What breastmilk looks like

Over the years, on the road from girlhood to womanhood, you have probably thought a lot about your breasts: their size, their shape. In a culture obsessed with appearance, a woman's attitudes to her breasts can influence her feelings of femininity, self-esteem and even her posture. It is highly unlikely though that anybody told you that, no matter what their size or shape, your breasts are nothing short of miraculous.

Irrespective of how you felt about your breasts before pregnancy, the realisation that they can make milk to nourish your baby and the experience of breastfeeding can give you a new perspective on your body and its amazing abilities.

### doing what comes naturally

Breastfeeding is an instinctive natural function — not a science — and millions of women all over the world do it without ever referring to a book. In fact, millions do it without ever having learned to read.

However, in our culture, doing what comes naturally is not always easy. While a vast amount of knowledge is gained in some areas such as science and technology, other knowledge, more ancient and basic,

*Photograph by Susan D'Arcy*

is sometimes lost. The loss of this knowledge — knowledge that for millions of years has been vital to human survival — has meant a loss of confidence for mothers in caring for their babies, the loss of a vital source of nourishment and a loss of control over our own bodies.

Man may have walked on the moon, but in many parts of the world, the simple, womanly function of breastfeeding a baby may seem more difficult and fanciful than the moonwalk. Yet successful breastfeeding does not require any special equipment and costs nothing but time and patience, knowledge and support. Having a basic understanding of how breastfeeding actually works is a big step towards successful breastfeeding.

## Bountiful breasts

When you are pregnant, the focus is often on your growing belly. However, although the changes to your breasts may be less obvious to others, they are just as dramatic. For many women, swelling, sensitive or tingling breasts are the first exciting sign that they are pregnant. Your breasts will undergo several changes during pregnancy and after birth, not only in size but in appearance.

### pregnancy brings breast changes...

The breasts of any woman who has borne a child are different from those of a woman who has not, whether she breastfed or not. Glandular tissue proliferates and fat is mobilised in the breast during pregnancy, causing them to increase in size. It is this increase that causes the changes to the shape of the breast, not breastfeeding.

Although it varies greatly from woman to woman, chances are your breasts will not return to their original shape after pregnancy and breastfeeding. But if you wean gradually, studies have found that fat (which affects the size of the breast) is more likely to be redeposited in the breasts and help them to return to approximately the same size. Very flat chests can often be the result of lactation suppression or sudden weaning.

*Photograph by Calico Studios*

### ...and the birth brings more

When your milk 'comes in' your breasts usually feel very full and tight. The veins, which stood out as your pregnancy advanced, may look like a map of a complex system of waterways leading down to your nipple. Squeezing the areola may result in sprays of milk, and the free breast may leak while your baby is feeding from the other. It is easy to feel then, that your breasts are full of milk. However, only part of this initial fullness is breastmilk. The rest is a natural infusion of blood and tissue fluid within the breast as they go into full production.

As your breasts settle down and adjust the amount of milk they are making to the amount of milk your baby is taking, you will find that they no longer look or feel as 'full'. This does not mean that you are losing your milk, or that your breasts are not making enough milk. It means that your body has fine-tuned the delicate balance between demand and supply. As you continue to breastfeed, your breasts may not be much bigger than they were before your pregnancy and may not feel full at all, unless you miss a feed.

Motherhood is a time of great change, both physically and emotionally. Rather than be disappointed at the changes in your breasts, you may like to view them as a mark of your passage from womanhood to motherhood.

## The anatomy of the breast

Your breasts are made up of glandular tissue, supporting connective tissue and protective fatty tissue. The amount of fatty tissue determines the size of the breast, which is in turn largely determined by genetics. So your mother and grandmother will influence the size of your breasts — but not your ability to breastfeed. The milk-producing part of your breast is the glandular tissue. The shape and size of your breast has nothing to do with how much glandular tissue you have. A big-breasted woman may have a small amount of glandular tissue and a large amount of protective fatty tissue, while a small-breasted woman may have little fatty tissue and a lot of glandular tissue. You do not need a particular amount of glandular tissue to breastfeed. Women with a small amount of glandular tissue are still able to breastfeed successfully.

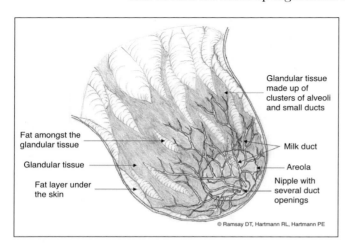

Glandular tissue made up of clusters of alveoli and small ducts

Fat amongst the glandular tissue

Glandular tissue

Fat layer under the skin

Milk duct

Areola

Nipple with several duct openings

© Ramsay DT, Hartmann RL, Hartmann PE

It is extremely rare for a woman not to be able to breastfeed. Even women who have had breast surgery often find that they are able to breastfeed with the right advice and support. In fact, there is no such thing as having the 'wrong' type of breasts, or the 'wrong' nipples. Women who have been told this simply have the wrong advice.

### all breasts have the same basic structure

While their size can vary enormously, all breasts have the same basic structure.

Each breast has approximately nine lobes of milk-making glandular tissue composed of clusters of alveoli, which contain the cells where breastmilk is produced. From this glandular tissue special channels called ducts run towards the nipple. It is from there that the milk flows out through tiny openings in the nipple.

The size and colour of the areola varies between women and contains special glands called Montgomery glands (those little bumps on your areola), which provide a natural lubrication, and which also help prevent bacteria growing on the nipples.

## Nipples

Your nipples play an important role in breastfeeding. They have smooth muscle that enables them to become erect in response to stimulation.

However, your baby needs to have more than just your nipple in her mouth to allow her to milk your breast. She needs to take a good mouthful of breast, enclosing much of the areola so that the large ducts below are between her jaws. Just chewing on your nipple will hurt you and frustrate her, as she will not get all the available milk.

When they are not erect, nipples usually look slightly flat, but when you are in contact with your baby, when you are cold, or when you are sexually aroused, they stand out. When your baby suckles, your nipple extends to form a teat, which is up to three times its original length. Each nipple contains anything from 4 to 18 (the average being 9) openings, or nipple pores.

### inverted nipples

Some women's nipples become erect easily. Others have to be coaxed out, and some seem to be flat or even go in instead of out. Nipples that go in rather than out are known as inverted nipples. If you have nipples like this you may need a little extra help to encourage them to stand out, but this doesn't mean you can't breastfeed. Your breasts and nipples can change dramatically throughout pregnancy so you may be surprised to find that nature has done her job and that your 'introverted' nipples have gradually become more 'extroverted' as your breasts grow.

## How breasts make milk

Understanding how your breasts make milk can help you to avoid or overcome some of the problems that have come to be associated with breastfeeding in the Western world.

Firstly, while you don't need abundant breasts to breastfeed, you do need a baby with an abundant appetite. A baby who feeds well and often is basic to a good milk supply. Fortunately, almost all babies are

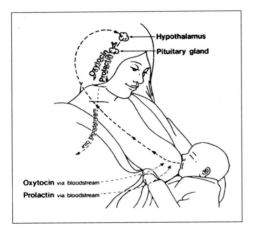

**Hypothalamus**
**Pituitary gland**

Oxytocin via bloodstream
Prolactin via bloodstream

born with a fundamental instinct known as the sucking reflex, and are keen to get started.

When your baby attaches to the breast and begins to feed, nerve impulses are carried to your brain, causing the release of hormones. One (prolactin) is involved in stimulating the milk-producing glands in the breast, while another (oxytocin) causes the 'let-down', or ejection of milk. It also lowers your blood pressure, heart rate and anxiety levels, while at the same time increasing insulin and blood glucose levels as well as your pain threshold, and has even been shown to decrease our resistance to performing repetitive tasks (a bonus only mothers could appreciate!).

*it's breastfeeding, not nipple feeding*

While breastfeeding, the nipple as well as a good mouthful of breast is drawn into your baby's mouth. Your nipple stretches as far back in his mouth as the junction between the hard and soft palate. (See page 44.) His tongue forms a trough around the nipple, so that the action of his tongue and jaw compresses the breast tissue and rhythmical, undulating tongue movements express milk into the back of his mouth.

If the nipple is not drawn to the back of your baby's mouth, it is liable to move around causing friction and then pain. You can test this effect by sucking your own thumb. The deeper the thumb is in the mouth, the less rubbing there is on the end of it. The type of sucking action a baby uses to 'milk' the breast is very different from the action he would use to suck milk from a straw or from a bottle teat.

## The let-down reflex

The skin covering the nipple contains nerve endings that are stimulated by your baby's initial rapid sucking at the start of a feed. The stimulation causes the milk to be released. This release is commonly called the let-down reflex (or the milk-ejection reflex).

The let-down reflex works something like a valve, or tap. It is this reflex that makes the milk your breasts have made available to your baby.

*a physical action...*

When your milk lets down, the cells surrounding the alveoli contract and squeeze out the milk, forcing it down the now expanded ducts towards the nipple. This process takes about 60 seconds. Some women feel it as a tingling sensation, or a sudden feeling of fullness. In the early days, you may also feel your uterus contracting when you let down, especially if this is not your first baby. This sensation is known as 'after-pains' and may be as strong as the early contractions you experienced during labour. Sometimes you may notice milk dripping from the other breast as you breastfeed. About 30 percent of women don't notice any of these signs, but all can see a change in their baby's sucking rhythm, from rapid little sucks to a slower drawn-up suck-and-swallow action, as the milk starts to flow.

### ...and a conditioned response

Just as your mouth may begin to water when you are hungry and smell something delicious cooking, the let-down reflex can also be triggered by the sight or sound of your baby, or even just by thinking about him. It can also be triggered by stimulation of the breast and nipple area by your fingers. Many people believe that, if you are very anxious, extremely tired, upset or in pain, your let-down may not work as well, but the truth is that mothers can cope with many different stresses and still breastfeed successfully.

The let-down reflex occurs an average of two or three times during each feed as the oxytocin is released in a pulsing manner throughout the feed, but most mothers will only notice the first let-down (if they notice it at all). Unless you're experiencing a problem with your milk supply, your let-down reflex is something you don't have to think about — it will just happen.

## Supply and demand

How much milk your breasts make depends on how often your baby breastfeeds and how much milk she takes. It is the removal of the milk by the baby that causes more milk to be produced.

A peptide, or special protein, found in breastmilk, regulates how much milk is made. As your breasts fill up with milk, the amount of this peptide builds up in your glandular tissue, so your breasts receive the message that nearly enough milk has been made and that they should slow down production. The more milk that is removed, either by your baby's feeding or when you express your milk, the lower the level of the peptide, so your breasts get the message to increase milk production. Each breast operates independently and produces different amounts of milk.

There is a big variation between mothers in the amount of milk they produce each day. Australian studies show a range of 500 to 1200 ml per day, the average being 800 ml, with the volume of milk remaining fairly constant from one to six months.

While the removal of milk from the breast is vital to the production of more milk for subsequent feeds, your breasts are never actually empty. Babies don't usually empty a breast — they stop feeding when they have had enough, while at the same time, your breasts are already at work making more. Studies measuring the amount of milk a baby takes show that about 65 percent of the available milk is used at each feed.

Despite slang references to breasts being 'jugs', your breasts are not at all like jugs of milk which can only hold a limited amount of fluid and which are obviously lighter and empty when the milk is poured from them. The human breast is more like the Magic Pudding, from the tale by Norman Lindsay. Whatever is eaten is automatically replenished, producing a constant supply, perfectly matched to need.

## What's in a breastfeed?

A breastfeed is like a long warm drink and a hot meal, all in one package. The fat composition of milk changes as the feed progresses. Milk at the end of a feed has a higher fat content than at the start of a feed.

It is important to allow your baby to set the pace of feeds, rather than timing them by the clock. A baby who is allowed to feed until she comes off the breast when she's ready receives the right balance of both nutrients and fats. If she is taken from the breast after only a few minutes, particularly in the early days when she may not be as efficient at milking the breast, she will only receive the warm drink, not the hot meal, and your breasts will receive the message that less milk is required and so will produce less.

The first milk that your breasts produce, colostrum, is high in immunoglobulins (or antibodies — factors which boost your baby's resistance to infection), lactoferrin (a component that both protects from infection and assists in the absorption of iron), chloride and sodium (salt)

*Photograph by Susan D'Arcy*

and low in lactose (milk sugar) and fat. It has a low volume, which causes minimal work for your baby's immature kidneys.

*tailor-made breastmilk*

Every mother's breastmilk is uniquely programmed to meet the particular needs of her baby. For example, the milk of mothers of premature babies differs from that of mothers of full-term babies.

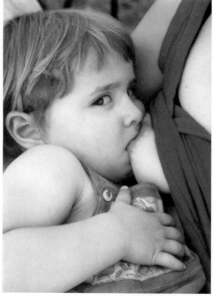

Mature breastmilk has higher concentrations of lactose and fat than colostrum, while its anti-infective properties remain the same, but are merely diluted by the increased volume of milk. You can feel confident that the overall protective levels remain constant and that breastmilk doesn't lose its nutritional value with time. In her first year, breastmilk is your baby's most important source of nutrition, even after you have introduced other foods.

Continuing to breastfeed past your baby's first year can be an important complement to her diet and can still provide vital protection from infection as she begins to have more contact with other adults and children. During weaning, your milk will begin to resemble colostrum again, with a greater proportion of sodium, protein and immunoglobulins, and less lactose. This is nature's way of giving your baby a final protective boost.

*Photograph courtesy of Katrina Matthews*

## What breastmilk looks like

We are so accustomed to seeing homogenised and pasteurised cows' milk, which is consistently white, that the appearance of breastmilk can come as quite a surprise.

Colostrum is a thick, yellowish fluid. You may have even noticed a little of it leaking from your breasts late in your pregnancy. After the first couple of days, and for the next week or so, your breasts will produce a cocktail of both colostrum and mature milk, making it look creamier than straight, mature breastmilk. If it has to be compared to the milk we are most familiar with, mature breastmilk looks a little like skim milk, but is more pearly and translucent, sometimes even a little bluish in colour.

The fuller your breasts, the bluer your breastmilk will look; the emptier your breasts the creamier your milk will look. Its fat content can vary with the time of day and the number of feeds your baby has had over that day.

## Sounds complicated?

If all this sounds very complicated, try to imagine a technical description of what happens when you eat — how the food is chewed in your mouth, the part your teeth play, how it is swallowed, the role of the oesophagus (food pipe), and how the food travels to the stomach and is digested. Sounds complicated — except that we do it without thinking, and enjoy it too.

The same goes for breastfeeding. Just as it is helpful to know about the digestive system when you need to treat problems associated with it, it will help you to resolve any breastfeeding problems you may encounter if you understand how breastfeeding works.

In most cases, neither you nor your baby needs to understand how breastfeeding works in order to do it successfully.

*When my brain made sense of breastfeeding, it seemed that my breasts and I did too! Most of the hiccups I encountered during breastfeeding may have been overcome or avoided with just a little knowledge.*

*Planning to breastfeed, asking lots of questions and listening to others' experiences will set you on your breastfeeding road to success.*

CHAPTER FOUR

# Preparing for breastfeeding

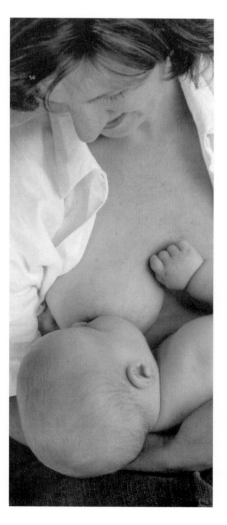

- *Learning-to-breastfeed classes*
- *All about the Baby Friendly Hospital Initiative*
- *Your options and choices for postnatal care*
- *Health professionals involved in care of new mothers*
- *The importance of support from your partner and others*

*It would have been helpful to personally know someone who I could call before I had problems.*

*Photograph by Susan D'Arcy*

From the day you announce your pregnancy, you will notice that apart from constant queries about 'What are you hoping for?', most of the focus will be on preparation for the birth.

While preparing for labour and birth are important, it is equally important, if not more so, to prepare for breastfeeding. Labour may last anything from one hour to 36 depending on how lucky you are, but a successful breastfeeding relationship can last for years.

It is ideal if your baby's entry into the world is as peaceful and loving as possible, but arriving safely is only the first step on the road to surviving and thriving. His journey throughout life will be a lot healthier and easier if he receives the best nurturing and nourishment that you can give him, and breastfeeding indisputably provides this.

So how can you prepare? One way is to read about breastfeeding and watch and talk to breastfeeding mothers. It is an old adage that knowledge is power and this applies to breastfeeding. The more you know about it from your own research, observation, and later, experience, the more confident you will be and the more likely to be successful.

Another way to prepare is to create a birth environment in which medical staff and support people support your decision to breastfeed and in which there is scope to be flexible and positive in a variety of circumstances. The right advice and assistance is important, especially in your baby's first few days.

## Learning-to-breastfeed classes

Most hospitals which cater for maternity patients conduct classes to help new parents prepare for the birth of their child. All antenatal programs have a breastfeeding education component; the most effective being

*Photograph by Yvette O'Dowd*

those offering separate breastfeeding classes that allow plenty of time for this vital subject.

Many Australian Breastfeeding Association groups offer breastfeeding classes at which you are guaranteed accurate, practical and empathetic information and ongoing support.

Breastfeeding classes can help you understand how breastfeeding works and give you the confidence in your body's ability to nourish your baby. They will explain why breastfeeding is important, how your breasts make milk, correct positioning and attachment and how to ask for and get help if problems occur. While you may have the opportunity to see a demonstration by a breastfeeding couple at a hospital-based class, you are certain to not only be able to watch a mother breastfeeding, but also be able to talk with her and ask questions (and perhaps her partner as well) at an Australian Breastfeeding Association class.

## Baby Friendly Hospitals

Most Australian women give birth in hospital — even some of those who planned a home birth. The hospital you choose therefore will play a big part in the establishment of breastfeeding.

In our grandmothers' day, the difference between giving birth at home and giving birth in hospital was chloroform. The mother was a patient rather than a participant in the birth, and the baby was delivered and packaged, stamped, labelled and sorted as efficiently as a parcel at a post office; blue for boys, pink for girls, all 'protected' from the germs of their parents and visitors behind a glass wall in the nursery. It was no

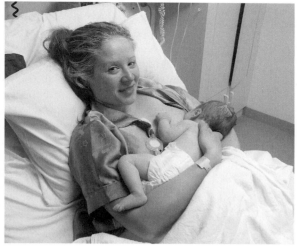

*Photograph courtesy of Paula Kimpton-Buob*

wonder that breastfeeding was often difficult under these circumstances. Separation of mother and baby meant the mother's breasts missed that vital stimulation of her baby's suckling and her milk would have been slower to 'come in'. The rigid feeding schedules of the day would also have inhibited the mother's milk supply as the amount of milk made depends on the stimulation of sucking.

These days, most Australian hospitals would class themselves as 'baby-friendly' in that they try to create the best possible environment for a baby's safe arrival and to ensure that the mother and baby are together as soon as possible after birth, so that bonding and breastfeeding can begin. Some hospitals have demonstrated their commitment by becoming accredited Baby Friendly hospitals and others are working towards this status.

### Ten Steps to Successful Breastfeeding

When this book was first published, in 1996, there were only two Australian hospitals which had been accorded official 'Baby Friendly' status, according to the criteria set down by the United Nations International Children's Emergency Fund (UNICEF) and the World Health Organization (WHO), to promote the *Ten Steps to Successful Breastfeeding* for optimal infant health. By the beginning of 2006 there were 52 accredited Baby Friendly hospitals in Australia.

### accredited hospitals must follow best practice

Hospitals that have Baby Friendly accreditation recognise that active support of breastfeeding requires much more than just allowing babies access to their mothers. An accredited hospital must follow best practice. For example, mothers are actively informed about the benefits of breastfeeding and are encouraged to breastfeed. Infant formula is not offered unless the mother clearly chooses to use it, or there is a compelling health reason (and even then the mother must give signed permission).

All nursing and midwifery staff members at Baby Friendly hospitals are expected to be knowledgeable about breastfeeding, and to attend professional development programs several times a year.

A Baby Friendly hospital is also likely to have breastfeeding classes separate from basic antenatal classes where the focus is on the birth. Many hospitals, both those designated as Baby Friendly and others, also have breastfeeding clinics where lactation consultants can help both inpatients and outpatients with any breastfeeding problems.

In Baby Friendly hospitals, if complementary feeds are necessary, where possible it will be breastmilk which will be given by cup or spoon rather than bottle, so that the baby does not become confused between the two different types of sucking.

Baby Friendly hospitals also recognise the importance of human contact in the progress of premature and sick babies and may encourage both staff and parents to carry these babies around in specially designed slings.

Infant formula is not banned, but neither is it supplied. Mothers who wish to use infant formula usually have to purchase and prepare their own. This includes the disinfection of bottles and mixing of the formula. This makes good sense, as careful hygiene and correct measuring is vital to ensure the safety of artificial feeding, and it is best that parents who wish to feed this way learn to do so properly.

The policy in Baby Friendly hospitals is that a mother should decide how she will feed her baby, but her decision should be an informed one. Despite some claims that such hospitals are not 'mother-friendly', a Baby Friendly policy does not mean that a mother would be forced to breastfeed against her wishes.

Making infant-formula-feeding a compromise rather than a choice between equals is not fanatical or unfair. It merely acknowledges the undisputed scientific fact that breastmilk is the *normal* food for babies, with all alternatives as inferior.

*The Ten Steps to Successful Breastfeeding*, developed by WHO and UNICEF are

1  Have a written breastfeeding policy that is routinely communicated to all health care staff.

2  Train all health care staff in skills necessary to implement this policy.

3  Inform all pregnant women about the benefits and management of breastfeeding.

4  Help mothers initiate breastfeeding within a half hour of birth.

5  Show mothers how to breastfeed and how to maintain lactation even if they should be separated from their infants.

6  Give newborn infants no food or drink other than breastmilk, unless medically indicated.

7  Practise rooming-in — allow mothers and infants to remain together — 24 hours a day.

8  Encourage breastfeeding on demand.

9  Give no artificial teats or pacifiers (also called dummies or soothers) to breastfeeding infants.

10  Foster the establishment of breastfeeding support groups and refer mothers to them.

## Hospital discharge policies

While discharge policies vary from hospital to hospital, many maternity units have a policy of discharging mothers who have uncomplicated deliveries within three days after the birth, while mothers who have had a caesarean are sent home on day five. With this in mind, a hospital that actively supports breastfeeding is doubly important.

This policy suits many women — after all pregnancy and childbirth are not illnesses — and many mothers feel more comfortable at home and are well enough to manage. Some studies have shown that early discharge doesn't adversely affect breastfeeding outcomes. At the same time, many mothers report feeling apprehensive about leaving a supportive environment before they get the hang of breastfeeding.

Breastfeeding is not fully established until sometime between 36 and 72 hours after birth, so leaving hospital beforehand means that there is usually no-one close at hand who can offer skilled help. Positioning and attaching a baby on a very full breast, once your milk comes in, can be very different from before, when your baby was receiving colostrum and your breasts were smaller and softer.

Hospital-based and community postnatal services vary from state to state, so ask your hospital about its postnatal services and check with your local council before you have your baby. Does your hospital provide midwife outreach visits to recently-discharged mothers? Is there a lactation clinic, a mother-baby postnatal unit or day-stay centre? What options are provided by the local child health service? If you know exactly what postnatal services are available to you, it will be a lot easier to find help quickly if you need it.

*Photograph by Helen Tidy*

## Birth centres

Some hospitals have birth centres where you can give birth in the comfort of a home-like environment, but with the security of medical intervention nearby if you should need it.

You, your partner, midwife and support people are in control. The advantage of a birth centre to the breastfeeding mother is that there is a less regimented and more relaxed environment where it can be easier to give your baby her first feed and get to know her at your own pace.

However, the policy in most birth centres is for very early discharge, so it is important that you arrange to receive breastfeeding support, either from a visiting lactation consultant, your midwife or your child health nurse for when you are discharged. Alternatively, you may like to ask about the possibility of moving into the postnatal ward after you leave the birth centre, if you are concerned that you are not ready to cope at home without support.

If you are planning a home birth, arrange for your midwife to be on hand to support you as you begin breastfeeding and for some ongoing help until you feel confident.

## Your doctor

Your choice of doctor or obstetrician may also affect your breastfeeding relationship with your baby. Studies show that a woman's chance of breastfeeding can be influenced, either positively or negatively, by her doctor's attitudes to breastfeeding. In fact, unsupportive or neutral doctors' attitudes have been firmly linked to early cessation of breastfeeding.

Discuss your commitment to breastfeeding early in your antenatal visits and enlist your doctor's support in preparation and referral to breastfeeding classes and helpful organisations. Make sure that your doctor understands and accepts that you wish to breastfeed as soon as possible after birth. Even if you are well during your pregnancy, and don't foresee any emergencies such as a caesarean delivery, it's a good idea to talk to your doctor about what can be done to ensure a good start to breastfeeding if things do not go as planned.

*Photograph by Yvette O'Dowd*

## Lactation consultants

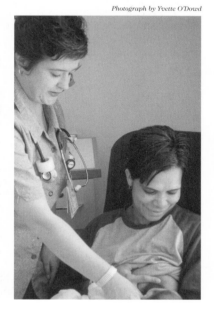

At some point in your breastfeeding experience, you may need to call on the services of a lactation consultant.

Most good maternity hospitals and birth centres employ lactation consultants whose job it is to get breastfeeding off to a good start and to solve any early problems that might arise. You may also have access to a lactation consultant through any post-discharge program that is offered by your birthing facility or through breastfeeding clinics. You might find that your child health nurse, or even your GP, is also a lactation consultant. Outside of the hospital and infant health system, there are a number of lactation consultants in private practice who see mothers on a fee-for-service basis.

Lactation consultants are allied health professionals who possess the necessary skills, knowledge and attitudes to facilitate breastfeeding. They offer support and specialist assistance to mothers who wish to succeed at breastfeeding, or who have problems that have not been resolved by other health professionals.

An International Board Certified Lactation Consultant (IBCLC) has passed a fully-accredited examination set by the International Board of Lactation Consultant Examiners (IBLCE). The IBCLC certification is recognised as the gold standard for health professionals working with breastfeeding women.

To find a lactation consultant in your area, see their professional association websites — Australian Lactation Consultants' Association at: http://www.alca.asn.au and the Network of Australian Lactation Colleges at: http://www.lactation.org.au. If you don't have access to the Internet, then your child health centre may be able to provide you with the names of lactation consultants. You can also phone the Australian Breastfeeding Association's Lactation Resource Centre or an association counsellor on the local Helpline in your state for details.

*Photograph by Prue Carr*

## Your partner

While the right birth environment and doctor are important, and other mothers will be invaluable for friendship and support, a vital source of support should be your partner, if you have one. This is why it is important for him to also be well-informed about breastfeeding.

Encourage him to read this book and any other material you would like to share with him, and talk to him about your discoveries and feelings about breastfeeding.

He may have equally strong feelings about your desire to breastfeed your child. He may feel proud, fascinated and passionate about it, or even a little envious; or he may feel concerned about whether you will be able to produce enough milk and whether breastfeeding will be tiring for you. He may have heard about other women who had difficulty breastfeeding or fathers who felt excluded from the closeness between a breastfeeding mother and child.

Apart from talking about his feelings with you, he might also like to talk to his friends or workmates about how they felt when their partners were breastfeeding and about what they did to support the breastfeeding relationship, including emotional and practical support.

*an invaluable support*

Your partner can be an invaluable support at the time of your baby's birth, especially if you need more medical intervention than you had hoped for. In this situation, you may be too exhausted to be assertive about wanting to breastfeed your baby as soon as possible after birth. This is where your partner or support people can step in, if necessary, to help ensure that your wishes are respected.

## A breastfeeding mentor

Having a breastfeeding mentor, someone to call on who can help and support you as you and your baby learn to breastfeed, can be invaluable. Ideally, this would be someone who has successfully breastfed (that doesn't mean that she never had problems), who understands what you are experiencing, and with whom you feel comfortable. It should be someone who knows how breastfeeding works and who is available to you, either by phone or in person during those vital early weeks. You won't need to be on the phone to her day and night, but it can be reassuring to know that help is at hand if you need it.

In a recent survey of mothers by the Australian Breastfeeding Association, participants said that, in hindsight, one of the things they most wished they had done was to make personal contact with a breastfeeding support group before their baby's birth. That way, they would have had someone to call on whom they already knew and with whom they felt comfortable.

*It would have been helpful to personally know someone who I could call before I had problems, as it would have been easier to make that phone call for help.*

Before your baby arrives, you may like to contact the Australian Breastfeeding Association for details of counsellors in your neighbourhood. You can go along to meet them and other mothers at local activities, or attend any learning-to-breastfeed classes that are being offered. By the time your baby is born, you will have a ready-made cheer squad. Even if you can't manage it before your baby is born, be sure to contact one of the association's local breastfeeding counsellors and go along to a group activity to see what support is available.

*Photograph by Yvette O'Dowd*

CHAPTER FIVE

# How to breastfeed

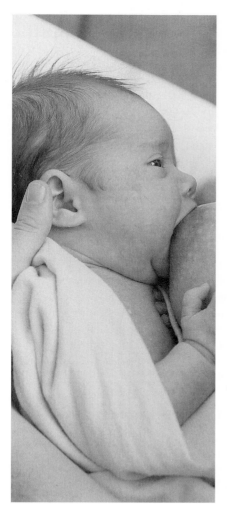

- *Positioning and attachment are important*
- *Steps in attaching your baby to the breast*
- *How often and how long to breastfeed your baby*
- *How to tell if you have enough milk*

*When you feel so sure of yourself that you could almost breastfeed swinging from a chandelier, it will be because you have the basic technique down pat.*

Photograph by Davina Hurst

It can be hard to imagine, as you fumble your way through those first breastfeeds, holding your breath in nervous concentration and excitement, that you'll soon be so confident that you will be breastfeeding without even thinking about how to do it.

The first step in reaching that point is for you and your baby to get the fundamentals right. Later, when you feel so sure of yourself that you could almost breastfeed swinging from a chandelier, it will be because you have the basic technique down pat.

You've seen the real estate advertisements? When it comes to buying a home, position is everything. A house in the right position will guarantee a return on your investment. The same goes for a breastfeeding baby. You'll read and hear a lot about 'positioning and attachment' as you learn more about breastfeeding. When we talk about positioning in breastfeeding, we are talking about how you bring your baby to your breast and position him to ensure that he is able to properly attach or latch on to your breast, feed effectively and get as much of the available breastmilk as he needs.

## Step-by-step guide to breastfeeding

*Feeding lying down*

*Photograph by Susan D'Arcy*

### 1. Make yourself comfortable

You can feed your baby while sitting or lying down, whichever feels right for you. If you'd prefer to lie down, you might find it more comfortable to use a couple of extra pillows to tuck under your shoulder or behind your back. Lie on your side, with your body slightly curved so that your baby can snuggle in next to you. If you're sitting up, you can use pillows to support your back, and you might find it easier to have a pillow on your lap to bring your baby's mouth level with your nipple (don't bring him up too high though).

### 2. Remove obstacles between you and your baby

Make sure your clothes (including your bra) don't restrict your baby's close contact with, or your view of his attachment to, your breast. Clothes that unbutton to the waist make it easier. You may even like to remove t-shirts or other tops as you learn to breastfeed, rather than tuck them under your chin. The last thing you want is to have to struggle with folds of clothes when you're concentrating on getting your baby attached to your breast.

Wrapping your baby snugly to keep his hands out of the way may not allow him to be close enough to attach comfortably. Unwrapping him, and tucking his lower arm around to your side, will allow him to get much closer.

*Photograph by Lesley McBurney*

*Cradle hold*

### 3. Position your baby to attach to your breast

Turn your baby onto his side, his mouth in line with your nipple. Using your hand, support him behind his shoulders and neck (not his head). Pull your baby in close to you, aligning his body at a slight angle to you with his chin closer to your breast than his nose. His whole body should be turned towards you so that his hips, tummy and chest are against you. Make sure that his mouth and nose are directly opposite your nipple.

*Photograph by Lesley McBurney*

*Photograph by Katie Sheldrick*

**Some alternative holds**

*Left: Modified cradle hold*

*Right: Underarm (football) hold*

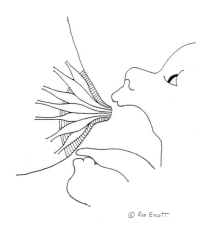

© Ros Escott

**Approaching attachment**
*Baby has wide gape with tongue down and forward. Nipple is aimed at the roof of baby's mouth, with first point of contact being baby's lower jaw or chin on the areola, well away from the nipple.*

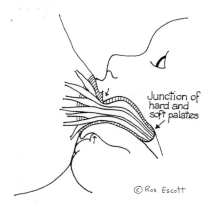

Junction of hard and soft palates

© Ros Escott

**Optimal attachment**
*Baby draws nipple and breast tissue back to the soft palate. Tongue is forward over gums, lower lip rolled out, chin against breast. Jaws are positioned well over the ducts and can compress them efficiently.*

*Adapted and updated, with permission, from article by Ros Escott, Breastfeeding Review, May 1989.*

## 4. Encourage your baby

Gently brush your baby's mouth with your nipple and the underside of your areola. Wait for him to instinctively nuzzle and open his mouth wide to gape for your breast. His natural rooting reflex will help him find the nipple. Some mothers find it helps to support the breast until they become more confident. Avoid moving or lifting your breast, chasing his mouth with your nipple. Try to keep your nipple in its natural position (where it would be if unsupported by your hand). A rolled up towel under the breast may help to lift the breast so that you can see the nipple, but still not change the natural position of your breast or nipple.

## 5. Bring your baby to your breast

When his mouth is wide open, and his tongue is well forward over his bottom gum, you can bring your baby quickly but gently to your breast. Aim the nipple towards the roof of his mouth, guiding it over his tongue, so that he will have not only the nipple but also a good part of the breast in his mouth before he can close it. It is important that the baby takes in as much of the nipple and areola as possible, with the greatest part being on the chin side of the nipple.

# Positioning and attachment checklist

When your baby is well positioned and attached:
- ❍ Her mouth will be right over the nipple and well onto the areola.
- ❍ Her tongue will be well forward cupping the nipple and areola.
- ❍ She will have more of the chin-side of the areola in her mouth than the side nearest to her nose.
- ❍ Her top and bottom lips will be turned out (flanged) over the breast.
- ❍ Her chin will be pressed against the breast.
- ❍ Her head will be tipped back a little.
- ❍ Her nose will be clear so that she can breathe easily.

 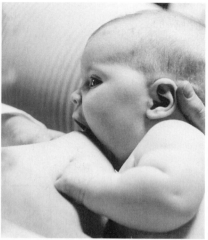

*Photographs by Katie Sheldrick*

(You shouldn't need to hold your breast away from her nose. Doing this may pull the nipple from her mouth or even block the milk ducts below your finger. If her nose is pushing into your breast, try moving her body and legs closer to you. This will bring her chin further towards the breast and free her nostrils naturally.)

○ She will be close enough to you so that she doesn't have to strain to hold on to the breast.

○ Your breasts won't feel painful beyond the initial stretching of your nipple.

(If it hurts, place a clean finger in your baby's mouth at the corner to break the suction, remove your nipple from her mouth and start again.)

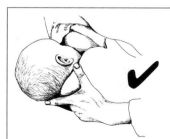

*Supporting her behind her shoulders will help you position her correctly*

*Pushing her head onto the breast may mean her nose makes contact before her chin.*

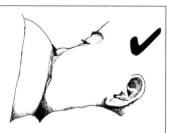

*Good attachment*

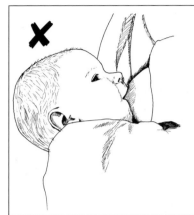
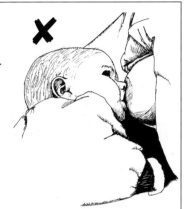

*Left: This baby's lower lip is not opened out over the breast. She does not have a good mouthful of breast.*

*Right: This baby is not close enough to the breast. Her chin is not touching, her nose is burrowed into the breast.*

## How often, how long, and will it be enough?

The three most frequently-asked questions that new mothers have are 'How can I tell if I have enough milk?', 'How often should I breastfeed?' and 'How long should a feed last?'

'You're not feeding again, are you?' Comments like this are not uncommon from people who are not used to breastfed babies. You may be warned that feeding every two hours, or topping up after 20 minutes, or an hour, will make your baby sick, fat, spoiled or worse still, it will be a sign that your milk is not 'good enough'. Fortunately none of this is true. By feeding your baby frequently you will ensure that you have enough milk to nourish your baby, and that she receives the comfort and security that she needs. Your milk is extremely well absorbed by your baby and unlike cows' milk, will not take long to digest. Her stomach is very tiny (about the size of her clenched fist) so it doesn't take much to fill it. Between four and nine weeks all babies feed during the night and from 9 to 26 weeks at least 60 percent of babies feed during the night.

### little babies feed very often

The fixation that the gold standard for spacing of infant feeds four-hourly is an obstacle to successful breastfeeding that has proven almost impossible to overcome. A four-hour gap between breastfeeds is at the extreme low end of the breastfeeding count, particularly for the first few months. Six four-hourly feeds in 24 will not usually provide enough breast stimulation and drainage and is often a recipe for poor supply, an unsatisfied baby and early weaning.

Research (and experience) has shown that, in their first couple of months, babies feed between 8 and 17 times in a 24-hour period, with the average being 11 times. Few babies younger than about three months sleep for long periods between feeds and if they do, this will be balanced by a period of more frequent feeding. Ideally, you should feed your baby whenever she displays common feeding cues such as restlessness, turning her head from side to side searching for the breast, opening her mouth and sucking her hands. Remember that crying is the very last sign that your baby wants to be fed, not the first.

*every baby is different*

Some babies like to linger over dinner, while others like to eat and run, so to speak. Some are enthusiastic and even ravenous feeders, while others are quieter or fussier. The frequency of your baby's feeds is best regulated by her, not by other people's expectations. Imagine how you would feel if someone told you when and for how long you could eat — probably hungry and frustrated. Some people call this baby-led feeding routine 'demand feeding' but experienced mothers know that it is really feeding according to need.

Let your baby feed from one breast until she stops actively feeding and either lets go of the nipple or falls asleep. If she is awake and interested, offer the other breast, again for as long she wants. Some babies are content to feed from only one side per feed in the early weeks, gradually needing to feed from both breasts at most feeds. During the time you are feeding from only one breast, make sure you balance the feeds so that each breast receives the same amount of stimulation. This will ensure you maintain your supply balance and prevent engorgement.

## How to tell if you have enough milk

*1. Wet nappies*

Based on the principle that what goes in must come out, after day three to five your baby should have at least six to eight very wet cloth nappies in 24 hours, provided no other fluids or solids are being given. If you are using single-use nappies, particularly those containing moisture-absorbing gel, you should expect about five nappies in 24 hours. However, the nappies should feel heavy after use. Over the first three or four days, urates may leave a rusty, orange-red stain on the nappy. This is perfectly normal during this time, but if you see staining on your baby's nappy later than this, it's usually a sign that he is not getting enough breastmilk.

### 2. Bowel motions

In his first 48 hours, meconium will make your baby's stools look dark and sticky. Over day three to four, his stools will change to a greenish brown-yellow, and from about day five they will look like yellow mustard curds. For the first week or so, he may have a bowel motion at each nappy change. Then over the next few weeks, he will probably have two or more soft bowel motions a day. Infrequent (that is, not daily) bowel motions in a very young baby usually suggest he needs more breastmilk. As the weeks go by your baby may have fewer soiled nappies, varying from baby to baby from daily to once or twice a week. It's all normal as long as the stools are soft and unformed.

### 3. Skin tone

Your baby should have a healthy skin colour relative to his ethnic makeup and good skin tone. (If you gently 'pinch' his skin, does it spring back into place?)

### 4. Behaviour

Your baby should be alert and reasonably contented for some periods in the day, even if he has some fussy or very unsettled times as well. He will usually wake for night feeds. A tiny minority of babies sleep for a lengthy period during the night, while the majority wake during the night for quite some time. It's very important to realise that 'sleeping through' in young babies is defined as sleeping for five hours!

*Photograph by Cath Palmer*

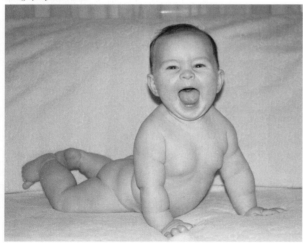

### 5. Growth

There should be some weight gain and growth in length and head circumference. This might not mean piling on a set amount of weight every week, but gradual weight gain spread across each month. Racial and family patterns can be factors in this growth pattern. Birth weight can also be a determinant — a baby does not necessarily stay on the same growth curve according to his birth weight. A large newborn may 'grow down' to his genetically-determined growth curve over the first year. Slow weight gain is more likely in a family where the parents are of small stature. However, a baby should show consistent growth over the first year. (See Chapter Twelve for more on weight gains.)

## Sleepy babies

Some babies may appear very undemanding; they consistently sleep for several hours and have little active awake time. These babies should be woken for feeds so that they will continue to gain weight. A good rule of thumb is to make sure an undemanding baby feeds *at least* three-hourly during the day, and *at least* once during the night.

On the other hand, some colicky babies seem far from content, yet continue to gain weight steadily. Colicky babies can be miserable and want to feed constantly. (See Chapter Fourteen for further information.)

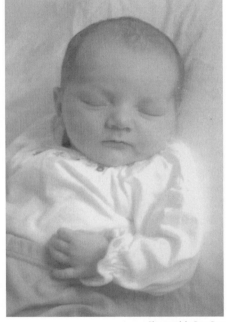

*Photograph by Prue Carr*

CHAPTER SIX

# Getting started

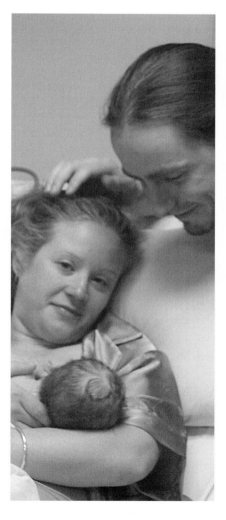

- *Skin-to-skin contact right from birth will encourage breastfeeding*

- *Dealing with early problems such as engorgement, sore nipples and jaundice*

- *What to do if your breasts leak milk*

- *Your feelings as a new mother*

- *Your baby is unique*

*I loved the serenity of being able to sit, undisturbed, just gazing at my beautiful baby and marvel at his very being.*

*Photograph courtesy of Paula Kimpton-Buob and James Buob*

The birth of your baby is arguably the most exciting, challenging and magical experience of your life. You'll still be on a roller coaster of emotions when it's time for you both to try another — the first breastfeed. Ideally, your baby's first feed will be as soon as he shows he is ready after his birth — usually within the first hour. Studies have shown that a newborn baby is often at his most alert and responsive at this time, and has a strong urge to suck (you may have even seen photos of babies in the womb sucking their fingers). And it's also been shown that getting off to a good early start means you will be more likely to be successful long term. Your baby will prefer the warmth of your body and the familiar sound of your heartbeat to any heated crib, and he will certainly feel a lot better about having his first bath if he has had the reassurance of your breast and your arms first.

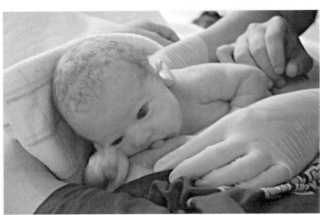

Photograph by Prue Carr

### ask that your baby stay with you

As soon as he is born, have your baby placed on your chest, skin-to-skin, while he recovers from the birth and begins to get to know you 'on the outside'. Skin-to-skin contact is vital for all babies. It helps maintain temperature, reduces their oxygen requirements, regulates heart rate and puts them in-sync with their mother's body flora. It also makes both mother and baby calmer and, of course, enhances communication and bonding between mother and baby.

If the room is cool, a blanket over both of you will ensure that he doesn't get chilled. A newborn baby is programmed by nature to crawl (wriggle) and seek the breast and attach. Watching your baby respond in this way is a truly amazing experience. These inborn instincts imprint his natural breastfeeding skills, minimising the chances of later problems with attachment.

## A reluctant starter?

Drugs administered to a mother during labour can affect her baby's natural sucking reflex, so some babies are not ready to feed right away. If possible, keep your baby close to you.

Allow your baby enough unhurried time and wait for cues of readiness, such as his turning his head from side to side with his mouth open, as he searches for your breast.

You could also try offering some gentle encouragement. You can express a little colostrum by squeezing the areola firmly about 30 mm back from the nipple and let a few drops fall into your baby's mouth. Sometimes, this first taste is enough to awaken interest or to help a reluctant baby to persist and try to latch on.

Don't force your baby or get frustrated yourself. Gently encourage his natural instincts. Even if your baby only feeds for a few minutes, you are both off to an excellent start. He will have received valuable nutrients and antibodies from your colostrum, as well as the reassurance that life outside your womb is likely to be just as warm and secure as it was inside it.

## Do not disturb

During the first few breastfeeds, you will probably prefer some privacy as you and your baby discover each other and breastfeeding. Make sure that staff or visitors are alerted to your need for this by hanging a sign on your door and keeping it firmly closed. If someone still persists by knocking or opening the door, don't feel shy about politely asking them to wait outside or to return at a more convenient time. If you're sharing a room, just draw the curtains around your bed when you want to concentrate on feeding. The other mothers in your room will probably want the same privacy and won't be offended.

*I loved the serenity of being able to sit, undisturbed, just gazing at my beautiful baby and marvel at his very being.*

Getting your baby feeding well and building your confidence in breastfeeding are the most important things at this stage. You will have plenty of time to catch up with friends later. Most people understand that this is a special learning time for you and your baby.

# Some first week issues

In the first week, you will be confronted with a number of issues — many of which are common and most of which are no cause for concern. If you know a little about what to expect, you will be more likely to take them in your stride.

## Engorgement

The breast size that you (or your partner!) may have sometimes fantasised about may not actually be ideal in practice if it means that your breasts are suddenly uncomfortably full and tight. Engorgement is caused not only by the increased volume of milk but also by the increased blood supply to the breasts, needed to begin milk production.

You will minimise engorgement if you feed your baby often (at the very least, eight times in 24 hours, but more often 10 to 12 times), very importantly, with some of those feeds being at night, ensuring he is correctly attached each time.

Engorgement makes it difficult for the nipple to protrude. If your breasts are so engorged that your nipples look quite flat, express a little milk before attaching your baby. This will soften the breast around the nipple and areola, making it easier for him to latch on.

*I found it really hard to sleep on those painful lumpy breasts, so I gazed hopefully down on my little one in her crib, hoping she would wake up, have a little feed and take some of this pain away — enough for me to get some sleep too.*

### engorged breasts can be hard to express

Engorged breasts can be hard to express. Using warm compresses before a feed, expressing a little milk under a warm shower, stroking the breast from the chest wall towards the nipple, all help if you need to express to make yourself comfortable. Remember to handle your breasts with lots of TLC as they bruise more easily when they're engorged. Make sure your bra supports your breasts and is not too tight (you shouldn't be able to see marks from seams or edges).

Warm compresses before feeds and cold packs afterwards can help bring relief if your breasts are painfully full. Special breast pads containing reflective material can be slipped inside the bra to reflect body heat and soothe swollen breasts, or there are other warm and cold packs available through pharmacies. The humble face washer wrung out in warm water for heat, and a bag of frozen peas wrapped in a damp cloth, make great low-cost alternatives.

Although research into their use is inconclusive, some women have found that thoroughly washed and dried, crisp, cold cabbage leaves, applied over the affected breast can provide relief. Remove any large veins in the leaves that could press on milk ducts. Avoid using the leaves over the nipples as cabbage may irritate some delicate skins.

If engorgement is causing you extreme pain, it may be helpful to express your breasts completely, once, either by hand or pump. You should talk to your medical adviser about pain relief if you find your engorged breasts unbearable.

When any initial engorgement subsides and breastfeeding becomes well established, your breasts will not feel this full and uncomfortable unless you have big gaps between feed times.

Photograph by Helen Tidy

## Night feeds

Before your baby was born, she received a continuous supply of food from you through the placenta and never knew what it was to be hungry. Once she is born, not only has your baby lost the warmth and support of your womb, she has a strange gnawing feeling inside that is caused by new and urgent feelings of hunger. Unlike an adult stomach, hers is extremely tiny (about the size of her clenched fist), so it doesn't hold much. Your milk is also extremely well absorbed by your baby, so it is easy to understand why she can't go long without being fed.

That is why you will need to feed your baby at night, as well as during the day. Most newborn babies need feeding several times throughout the night and this may continue for weeks or months, depending on your baby's individual needs. Night feeds are also important in establishing and maintaining your milk supply. While you are in hospital, having your baby's bed beside yours makes it easier to respond when she stirs for a feed. You'll quickly get to know her cues and it's not usually too long before you are both asleep again. You'll also be more comfortable and sleep better because your breasts are less likely to become engorged.

## Declining complements

Your baby will be well nourished by your colostrum for the first few days after birth, and if given the opportunity to feed frequently, will not need any other fluids. Most babies lose weight initially, and this is not an indication that they need anything other than breastmilk. Many mothers find their babies become increasingly unsettled in the 24 hours or so before their milk comes in and need to feed as frequently as every hour or more. This settles down once the milk comes in and seems to be a natural part of their development.

If your baby is unsettled for any reason, you may find that there are still hospital staff who suggest the use of a complementary feed (a top-up of infant formula or boiled water). It is very important to reinforce with staff that you are fully breastfeeding and that your baby does not need, and should not be given, extra fluids — including water and particularly not infant formula, unless there is a compelling medical need to do so.

Research shows that babies can lose more weight when given fluids other than breastmilk in the early days. Any foreign fluid will reduce his appetite and his desire to breastfeed and therefore inhibit your supply. If there is a family history of allergies, food intolerance or medical conditions such as asthma or diabetes, infant formula should only be given when prescribed by a paediatrician.

If your baby doesn't settle after a feed you can try putting him back to the breast for a top-up after 20 minutes or so. Your body is making milk all the time and your breasts are never completely empty.

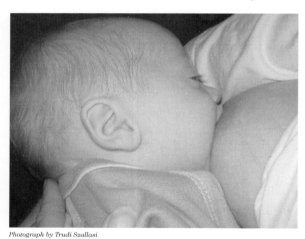

Photograph by Trudi Szallasi

*This baby is well positioned at the breast and well attached*

## Early nipple soreness

Sore nipples in the first week (or in fact at any time) can certainly take the enjoyment out of breastfeeding, but rest assured that this is usually short-lived. Some tenderness is common in the early days of breastfeeding when the nipples are naturally more sensitive, as they become accustomed to the strong sucking of a healthy baby. This initial tenderness is different from nipple pain experienced when a baby is poorly positioned and is consequently damaging the skin of the nipple.

Sometimes mothers are still advised to limit feeds in the early days to try to lessen any early discomfort. However this has been shown to merely delay the soreness. Restricting your baby's time at the breast also leads to a build-up of milk and increased engorgement, resulting in even further soreness. Most mothers find that sore nipples improve quickly once they become more skilled in attaching their babies correctly.

### your baby may take time to learn

Your baby is also learning how to breastfeed and may take time to learn how to milk the breast effectively. Don't hesitate to ask a lactation consultant or the midwifery staff at the hospital for help.

If pain persists after the first week or so, or your nipples become very sore, cracked, red, blistered or bruised, it is time to seek skilled help from an Australian Breastfeeding Association counsellor, a lactation consultant, child health nurse or your medical adviser.

### nipple tlc

Your skin is more easily damaged when it is either too dry or too moist, so keeping nipples healthy and supple is important in preventing soreness. If your breasts are leaking milk between feeds make sure that your bras and clothing don't become soggy. Breast pads (either single-use or washable) worn inside your bra can help absorb moisture and keep your nipples dry, provided they are changed regularly. Avoid using nursing pads that hold moisture against the skin.

It may help heal a damaged nipple if you express a little colostrum or milk onto it at the end of a feed, and then leave your bra open until it dries naturally or go without a bra sometimes. Don't use any drying agents; even soap can dry out the skin so that it is more prone to cracking. Nature provides the best lubricant during pregnancy and lactation, with special glands in the areola producing natural oils that clean and lubricate the nipples. Rinsing with water during your daily bath or shower is all that is needed.

## Weight loss

Babies may lose up to 10 percent of their birth weight in the first three days. This is normal and doesn't mean he needs other fluids, as long as he is given unrestricted access to your breast. He will be receiving valuable colostrum and stimulating your breasts to supply the mature milk that he needs after the first few days. Most babies gain weight from about day three, and regain their birth weight by the end of their second week; some take a little longer.

## Jaundice

If, by day three or four, your baby seems to be developing a deep olive or ochre complexion while the rest of the family are pink, white or freckly, don't fear a recessive gene, or worse still, that you have the wrong baby. It is likely that your baby has physiological jaundice.

Jaundice occurs when your baby's body is having trouble breaking down or getting rid of bilirubin, which is usually expelled through the liver or bound to albumin in the bloodstream. Bilirubin (a compound produced when foetal red blood cells are replaced by normal red blood cells) is yellow, which is why babies who are jaundiced look yellow.

Jaundice is a relatively common condition in newborn babies. It is estimated that between 30 and 75 percent of babies develop jaundice, which is generally a benign, temporary and easily-treated condition, not a disease. Physiological 'normal' jaundice appears on the third or fourth day, can be gone by the seventh day and usually requires no treatment.

Inaccurate feeding advice, such as limiting the amount of colostrum and breastmilk your baby receives in the first few days can be a factor in this type of jaundice. Breastfeeding helps resolve jaundice as colostrum has a natural laxative effect that helps your baby to pass meconium and rid excess bilirubin from his body.

Breastmilk, rather than water, is the best way of reducing bilirubin levels, as this helps the baby's body pass the excess bilirubin out in the stools. Giving water can increase bilirubin levels as well as reducing your baby's desire for the breast and affect your milk supply. Babies affected by jaundice are usually very sleepy and need to be encouraged to feed more often.

### breastmilk jaundice

Very occasionally, a substance in breastmilk seems to cause jaundice (so-called 'breastmilk jaundice'). In otherwise healthy babies, bilirubin levels rise on the fourth to seventh day and peak at two weeks then slowly drop to normal at between 4 and 16 weeks. No treatment is usually required, but phototherapy may be recommended if bilirubin levels rise above a certain limit. This may not be evident until after you and your baby are discharged from hospital, so it is important to keep a close watch on his yellowness. Your baby may need to be readmitted to hospital for treatment, or to be reassessed to rule out other more serious causes of jaundice. In occasional cases, you may also be advised to stop breastfeeding temporarily, to express milk and feed him an alternative milk until the bilirubin levels reduce somewhat.

## Leaking

Leaking breasts, especially in the early days when your milk comes in, is a common problem for many breastfeeding mothers. This usually settles down as the sphincter muscles at the tip of the nipple develop and exert more control over the outflow of milk.

Meanwhile, there are several things you can do to reduce the discomfort and inconvenience of having milk stream onto your clothes and bedding.

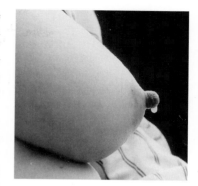

○ Try bathing your breasts several times a day alternately in very warm and cold water. This sometimes increases the blood circulation to the breasts, improving their tissue tone so that leaking subsides.

○ Cover your nipples with nursing pads tucked into your bra. Make sure your bra is roomy enough for this. You can buy washable nursing pads, or single-use ones, or make your own from old towels or linen. Avoid nursing pads that hold moisture against the skin, as they may result in soggy nipples that may become sore or cracked.

○ Use a clean nappy or other soft natural fibre cloth to catch any milk that pours out of one breast while your baby feeds from the other. Try not to use tissues or other synthetic fibres as these can be abrasive.

○ You might choose to wear your bra and nursing pads to bed, and perhaps use a mattress protector if you are leaking during the night, or you may prefer to place nursing pads or other absorbent padding inside a closely-fitting vest, singlet or T-shirt. If you wear your bra to bed, take care that it doesn't cut in when you are lying down, because this might lead to blocked milk ducts.

○ If you need to stem the overflow of milk in certain circumstances, such as when you are breastfeeding away from home, press firmly on your nipple with your hand or forearm for several seconds after the let-down reflex starts. Crossing your arms can be a discreet way to do this. Try to not do this too regularly, as sometimes this too can cause blockages in the milk ducts.

## Not feeling motherly?

Rather than feeling elated, many mothers feel exhausted, overwhelmed and emotionally vulnerable after the birth of their baby. Rather than feeling motherly, they feel they need mothering themselves. It's natural to feel this way. As you care for your baby and get to know each other, you will usually find these negative emotions pass and are replaced by ones of love and protectiveness.

Breastfeeding is one of the best ways of overcoming these feelings, as the special hormones that are released when the baby suckles help relax you and enhance your motherly instincts. And while you are feeling ambivalent, you can be reassured that your baby will still be getting the best nourishment in the most comforting and loving way from you.

If you are worried about your feelings, it may help to talk to other mothers or to an Australian Breastfeeding Association counsellor. However, if negative feelings persist, it is wise to consult your doctor who may refer you to a specialist and to a postnatal support group.

Ongoing negative emotions may be signs of postnatal depression, especially if they are combined with isolation and lack of support. Postnatal depression is an illness that can not only make you feel miserable, but can affect your relationship with your baby.

### depression can take many forms

> *I absolutely clung to breastfeeding my baby. Breastfeeding was my 'rock'. Everything else was falling down around me in my depressed state, but I knew I could breastfeed.*

Depression can take many forms. Sometimes it causes a type of numbness in your heart that makes it impossible to find the energy to cope with caring for yourself, let alone another helpless person. At other times it can cause you to be angry and to feel that your baby is being unreasonably demanding and that it is you, not her, who deserves the loving care. Sometimes it can cause you to be overly anxious about your baby.

This is a serious problem for both you and your baby, if not treated. However, by talking about your feelings early on and getting skilled help when you need it, postnatal depression can be overcome. If your condition warrants it, your doctor may prescribe antidepressant medication. There are many antidepressants that are safe to use while breastfeeding.

If you need treatment at a clinic where you are required to stay overnight or longer, you can continue to breastfeed by taking your baby with you. That way you will still be providing the best care for your baby while you are getting vital care for yourself.

If you are affected by postnatal depression, it may help to know that it is caused by a number of factors and that it affects all types of women. Suffering from this illness does not mean you are a bad mother or will not be able to raise your child successfully.

## Changing needs, changing advice

Most women feel particularly vulnerable after the birth of a baby. Just when you need help most, it seems it is most difficult to ask for it. For a start, you may feel extremely emotional. In the first few days and weeks after giving birth, your hormones will be raging and you will find that your moods will swing from euphoria to despair and back again in a surprisingly short time. It is also a shock to find that while you may be extremely competent in other things, you feel extremely incompetent in dealing with your own baby. Even if you are familiar with babies, each one is different and you and your baby will be learning about each other. This can be like learning to dance. Sometimes it is hard to get the synchronisation right, even if you know the steps.

If you need help, remember that the staff, however busy, is there to help you. Asking for advice does not obligate you to follow it all. You may canvass a range of opinions, try the ones that you think will suit you and discard others that do not work.

Most hospitals employ lactation consultants who are employed to advise you and help you to establish breastfeeding. You will find that most are knowledgeable and sympathetic and many of course, are mothers themselves, and understand what you are going through.

*It was difficult with a newborn baby and painful breasts to organise to go and see a stranger about breastfeeding problems. I was lucky to find people I felt comfortable with, but also received lots of different advice. This was useful, as it gave me more options to try, but also frustrating while I was still learning and struggling.*

If you are asking for suggestions from relatives and friends, hopefully they will appreciate that you are trying to learn what suits you and your baby. While you welcome their suggestions, what worked for their children may not work for yours, so they should not feel offended if their advice is not taken.

## every breastfeeding relationship is unique

If the advice you have been given has not helped, don't be discouraged. Every breastfeeding relationship is unique and it can take a little time and patience to find the right solutions for you. You are the one who knows and understands your baby best. Listen to the 'experts', but listen to your own instincts too.

Even people who are supposed to know it all, such as breastfeeding specialists, are always learning new things about breastfeeding. The fact that this book has recently been revised is proof that everyone is still learning about breastfeeding, not just new mothers. When people give advice about breastfeeding, as in any other aspect of life, they are influenced by their own experiences, perceptions and values, so you will need to factor in this bias when you weigh up their suggestions.

It's also important to remember that the first few weeks and months of your baby's life are times of rapid change and until breastfeeding is established, the helpful advice you will need will change almost as rapidly as your baby grows. A baby's needs at one week are vastly different from those of a six-week-old baby, and these are different again from those of a six-month-old or a one-year-old.

## Going home

The only thing that you can be sure of when you have your baby is change. It seems that no sooner do you become accustomed to your baby's cues than she develops new and different ones. She is not doing this to deliberately frustrate you. Babies are people too, and like grown-ups, their behaviour changes according to their needs.

This can be a bit disconcerting at first. That tiny sleepy bundle that seemed content to just sleep and eat while you were in hospital,

*Photograph by Susan D'Arcy*

may seem to metamorphose when you return home into a ravenous and ranting monster. Suddenly, she seems to cry more often, even after she has been fed and changed, and you may feel unsure of how you can comfort her.

Don't worry. Your baby is growing rapidly. In her first year, she will grow at a greater rate than at any other time in her life. Babies take time to adapt to their environment and even small changes can cause them to react to this stress. At home, you may also have to resume other responsibilities and your baby may miss that 'cocooned' time in hospital, when she was your only responsibility and you were able to attend to her without delay.

You can offer the breast to satisfy both her appetite and her need for closeness, and at other times balance this with your own need to attend to other tasks by rocking and talking to her in soothing tones, and just letting her know that you are nearby. It may be difficult to believe at first, but as you get to know each other and her system matures, your baby and your life will become more predictable.

CHAPTER SEVEN

# Special deliveries

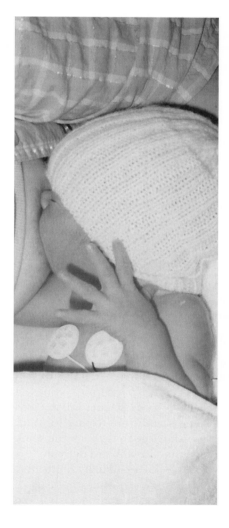

* Caesarean delivery
* Premature babies
* Twins
* Babies who are sick or have a disability

*Expressing for my babies allowed me to feel like their mother... Breastmilk was the only thing I could do for them as a mother.*

Photograph courtesy of Lian Tigani

Pregnancy is an important time for you to become accustomed to the idea of being a mother. As your baby grows, so you grow used to the idea of motherhood. Even though we know that things don't always go to plan, we imagine ourselves with the picture-perfect baby, a gentle unhurried birth and a smooth transition to parenthood.

That's why giving birth prematurely, perhaps by caesarean delivery, can be quite a shock. Finding out that you are expecting two babies (or even more!) may have you wondering how on earth you will cope. And, what we all dread the most — a very sick or disabled baby — sees our image of ourselves as a mother evaporate.

Breastfeeding can hold out a lifeline to you as you gradually come to terms with your new situation. Providing breastmilk is the one thing that only you can do for your baby or babies. It will be immensely important, not only to your baby's physical and emotional health, but to yours as well.

## Caesareans

If concern about you or your baby means that your doctor decides that a caesarean birth is safer for you both, don't let anyone persuade you that you can't breastfeed. While the timing and means of your baby's

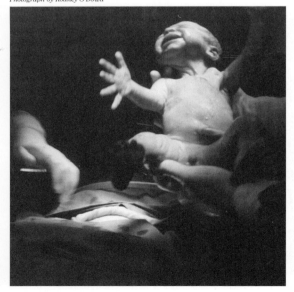

*Photograph by Rodney O'Dowd*

caesarean delivery may have short-term influences, you are no less likely than a mother who has given birth vaginally to be able to breastfeed.

Even if you get off to a slower start, studies show that you'll catch up before the end of your baby's first week.

### elective caesareans

If you know ahead of time and you are having an elective caesarean, you will have more time to prepare yourself emotionally and practically, and perhaps allow you time to talk to other women who have gone through the same experience. Babies who are delivered by elective caesarean are usually more alert regardless of the type of anaesthetic used. They usually have a stronger suckling action than babies born following an emergency caesarean delivery, where they may have undergone stress after a prolonged period of exhausting labour.

The type of anaesthetic your doctor uses will impact on your initial breastfeeding experience, so it's more usual to opt for a spinal or epidural anaesthetic, unless there is an emergency or a general anaesthetic is unavoidable. An epidural will mean that you will be conscious and alert throughout the birth. Mothers who are given an epidural can usually breastfeed soon after delivery. If you need a general anaesthetic, a pre-operative sedation is not usually given. This means that you may wake up more quickly once your baby is born.

Sometimes the drugs used during anaesthesia may temporarily cause your baby to be a little slow to initiate breastfeeding. You probably won't feel 100 percent yourself — after all, you will have just had major abdominal surgery! You will both need some time, patience and care while you recover from the delivery.

### not every caesarean mother can start breastfeeding immediately

Not every caesarean mother can start breastfeeding immediately, particularly if her baby is premature or unwell and needs time in special care. Even if there is a time lapse of several hours or even days before you put your baby to the breast, have confidence that it will work out in the end, despite a less-than-perfect start. You can ask for help with expressing your colostrum and, later, your breastmilk, if it comes in before your baby is able to attach to your breast. The staff will ensure that you and your baby spend as much time together as possible, despite any technological barriers.

For the first day or so, you will have a few attachments, which may include a catheter, a drain from your wound and an intravenous drip. While you're hooked up, you may need a little help with holding and positioning your baby at each breastfeed. If you're in pain, talk to the medical staff about an analgesic that won't make your baby sleepy or likely to suck less strongly. Feeling comfortable will improve your enjoyment of your baby and help your milk to flow — pain won't. You will be up and moving around as soon as possible, and the hospital physiotherapist can help speed your recovery by teaching you some postnatal exercises specially designed for caesarean mothers.

Breastfeeding while holding your baby across your body can be uncomfortable at first, so you might need to try several different positions until you find one that suits you both. See the section on twins that follows to get some ideas on other feeding positions.

Once you leave hospital, you will probably take a little time to return to your normal energy levels. Rest is very important — breastfeeding gives you a wonderful excuse to sit or lie down. Accept as much practical help as you're offered and ask for some if it isn't.

# Premature babies

If you confidently expected to carry your baby to term, giving birth prematurely will mean your life will be turned upside down. You may have planned to stay in paid work close to when your baby was due, or to relax at home in the last weeks or spend that time making arrangements for your baby's arrival.

When your baby arrives early, you will naturally be thrown. You may not be prepared physically or emotionally. The time you imagined as a period of contentment, slowly getting to know your baby may now be a period of high stress, especially if her prematurity means that she is unwell or needing special care.

A premature baby is one who is born three or more weeks earlier than the normal 40 weeks of gestation. You may also hear the term 'low-birth-weight baby'. This means a baby who weighs less than 2500 grams. These babies are mostly, but not always, premature, and need the same care as premature babies. These days, prematurity, while still a cause for concern, is no longer the worry it once was. Thanks to advances in specialist care and medical knowledge, babies as young as 22 weeks gestation have a chance of survival. Most premature babies, however, not only survive but thrive.

## 'Pre-term' milk — vital for premmies

Breastfeeding is a vital aid in your premature baby's survival. Because breastmilk is easy to digest, it is less taxing on her immature digestive system than any other food. Eliminating the small amount of waste will not overtax her immature kidneys. It will provide resistance to infections and in fact, the milk from mothers of premature babies has nutrients specific to their babies' developmental stage. 'Pre-term' milk, although similar in many respects to full-term breastmilk, contains higher concentrations of protein and some chemical compounds and minerals vital for premmie growth.

Even if your baby is in a humidicrib or special care nursery, there is no reason why she cannot receive your breastmilk (except if she is too immature for oral feeds). Some babies are fed intravenously for a while. The suck/swallow reflex is not always fully developed until somewhere between 32 and 40 weeks gestation, so it may take a while for your premature baby to actually breastfeed. Many premature babies receive their mother's expressed breastmilk through a feeding tube inserted into the stomach through either the nose or mouth until they are

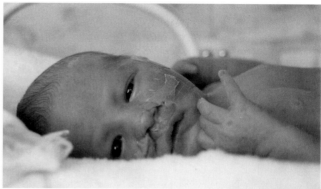

*Photograph by Lesley McBurney*

able to suck and swallow properly. Starting with tiny amounts, she will gradually receive more breastmilk. Sometimes parents are asked to assist with tube-feeds, so get involved when you can — it will give you confidence in handling your baby.

If your baby is being tube-fed, ask if you can have her near your nipple as she is being fed. She will soon start searching for your nipple and will hopefully latch on and suck. Sucking is important for all newborn babies and doing so while being tube-fed actually aids digestion.

The special care nursery will seem a very strange place, with lots of buzzing and beeping machines, doctors, nurses and humidicribs or incubators. Every time you see your baby, you may have to wash and put on a gown. Try not to be intimidated. Hospital staff welcome parents' involvement. You may like to bring a lambskin for your baby to lie on and something special to hang on her cot to make it seem more personal. Stroke or touch your baby as much as you can.

## Expressing

Until you can feed your baby directly from your breast, you will need to express your breastmilk. Even if you only manage to express a tiny amount each time, pre-term breastmilk has very concentrated nutrients, and your baby will benefit from every drop. Start expressing from your breasts as soon as possible after the birth to build your milk supply and to keep building on this supply in the early weeks, even if your baby is taking very little. Mothers of premature babies have found that establishing a full milk supply is important to later breastfeeding success. It's easier to maintain an established supply and to have enough milk for your baby as her appetite increases.

While freshly-expressed breastmilk is best for your baby — freezing and thawing change some components of the milk — thawed breastmilk is the next best food and ensures that you will always have breastmilk ready when she needs it, even if you are separated. Sometimes very tiny babies may need extra vitamins, iron and other nutrients added to their breastmilk. This does not mean your milk is inadequate. Your baby just needs a little boost because she is so very tiny. This is to make up for what your baby would have received in your uterus if she had not been born so early.

## Kangaroo care

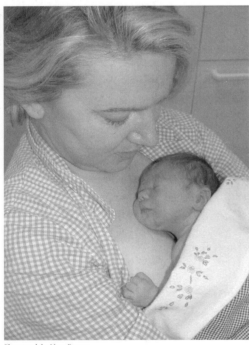

*Photograph by Mary Brown*

*Kangaroo care*

As your baby's condition stabilises, you may be offered 'kangaroo care', a method of caring for premature babies that allows them to be carried around in a special pouch, or just placed inside your shirt against your skin, while wearing only a nappy and perhaps a woolly hat. (The baby, not you!) This close contact with your body will help your baby maintain her own body temperature, stabilise her heart rate and breathing, and the contact with your breasts will encourage her to feed. In addition, this will improve both her sucking ability and your supply, due to an extra boost of hormones that occurs when mother and baby are in skin-to-skin contact. This method of interaction with premature babies has been found to increase a mother's expressed breastmilk supply by an average of one and half times. Sometimes you can even use kangaroo care while your baby is still attached to the ventilator. Fathers can also take part in this very rewarding special care.

## 'Real' breastfeeds

Your baby's first 'real' breastfeeds are an important part in her development. Once she starts to develop a mature sucking and swallowing reflex, is strong enough, and can control her body temperature (while you hold her close), she will be ready for this new adventure. You may start to notice pre-breastfeeding behaviour such as her licking her lips, trying to put her hand to her mouth, and waking and crying regularly for feeds.

Many babies go from tube-feeding to the breast without ever having bottles. Research has shown that breastfeeding is less stressful for premature babies than bottle-feeding. The sucking pattern of a premature baby differs from that of a full-term baby. She will generally start feeding with short bursts of sucking and then long pauses between active sucking periods. These could be rhythmic, slow sucking or fast, flutter sucking or a mixture of both. Don't expect too much at first — even if all that happens is your baby licks your nipples and has a few exploratory sucks, you are on your way. As she matures, her sucking periods become longer and her sucking more vigorous.

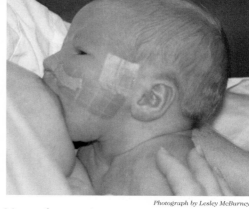

*Photograph by Lesley McBurney*

*Premature baby feeding at the breast for the first time*

Many premature babies have attachment problems, often due to a receding chin, under-developed cheeks and a small mouth. Don't be afraid to ask a hospital lactation consultant to help you with positioning and attachment. Premature babies have less fat in their cheeks than full-term babies, and this makes it harder for them to get a good grip on the breast. Sometimes, a thin nipple shield can make early breastfeeding attempts by weak, premature babies more successful.

## An anticlimax?

It can be very upsetting if you need to go home without your baby. You may still feel upset at the fact that your baby came into the world under stressful circumstances, and going home without her may intensify your feelings of loss and sorrow. It may help to focus on the more positive aspects of going home, such as having more time to sleep, to express, and to talk with your partner about your feelings. This may also give you time to make final preparations for your baby if she arrived very early.

When your baby finally comes home it may feel a bit like an anticlimax. The normal visitors and congratulations may be missing or people's reactions may be inhibited by their fear that inquiring about your baby's condition may be upsetting for you. Let them know that this is still a special occasion for you. Some parents feel that nobody really understands what they went through in hospital. If you feel like this, it may help to join a support group for the parents of premature babies, or to keep in touch with other parents from the special care nursery. Your local Australian Breastfeeding Association group can also offer a wealth of support and information.

## Twins

Photograph by Susan D'Arcy

Sometimes it takes a good nine months to get used to the idea of having one baby. The mother expecting twins therefore may be twice as excited — and twice as daunted. If twins are prevalent in your family (and it's often the case), you may be able to talk to other parents in the family about how they managed. You may wonder whether you really will be able to breastfeed both babies. Breastfeeding twins is both practicable and possible.

Remember that breastfeeding works on a demand-and-supply basis — the more milk that is taken, the more is made — so if you feed your babies frequently, you won't have any trouble providing plenty of milk for them.

If your twins are premature, weak or small, as some can be, breastfeeding is doubly important. If they are in the special care nursery, you may need to express your milk to establish your supply, preferably eight to ten or more times a day, including at least once at night. If only one baby is in care, you can try expressing from the 'spare' breast while the other baby is feeding, alternating breasts at each feed. The breastfeeding baby will trigger the let-down reflex, making it easier to express from the other breast.

### Separately or together?

You may be wondering whether to feed your babies together or separately, to keep each to his or her own breast, or to alternate sides. There is no one right way and the final decision is as much your babies' as yours. Most mothers interchange, depending on the ages and stages of their babies.

Some of the advantages of feeding separately:
- ○ It allows you to give plenty of attention to positioning and attaching each baby correctly, and is probably easier and more comfortable for you at first.
- ○ You will have more mobility, so it may be more practical if you have other children who need your attention during feed times.

The disadvantages include:
- ○ You may spend twice as much time feeding and it may feel as if you always have a baby at the breast.
- ○ If both babies need a feed at the same time, you will probably find it difficult to relax and feed while one is upset.
- ○ It can be difficult to settle one baby if the other is crying for a feed.

Some of the advantages of feeding both babies at the same time are:
- ○ It satisfies and calms both babies and is very relaxing once you have mastered the technique.
- ○ Usually one baby feeds from only one breast each time, so feeding may take even less time than for the single baby who feeds from both sides with a rest between sides. Some babies however may need more sucking time.

The disadvantages include:
- ○ It may take some experimentation to find the most comfortable feeding position and you might need another person to help with this in the first weeks.
- ○ Your babies may be quite different, both in weight and temperament, and have different feeding needs, so feeds won't always coincide. You might often have to wake the second baby to feed and not all babies feed well under those circumstances. Many babies, however, soon adapt and feed together happily.
- ○ In hot weather, you may find it oppressive to be surrounded by pillows and babies. A fan blowing near your face will help circulate the air and make you feel more comfortable.
- ○ Feeding in public places might be difficult unless you can find a suitable spot.

## Each to their own?

If you are giving each baby his or her own breast, there are a few other things to keep in mind.
- ○ If one baby does not suck as well as the other, you may find it best to alternate breasts to help the weaker baby.
- ○ Babies need equal right and left visual stimulation. If each baby always

feeds from the same breast, you should vary positions at that breast, for example from underarm hold to normal cradle hold. Carrying or burping babies in varying positions will also help.

○ Some women find that each breast has a differing ability to produce milk, so one baby may consistently get less. Of course this may be an advantage for babies with different appetites and if they are fed according to need, this won't affect the total intake over a day.

## Hold everything! I'm feeding

Breastfeeding twins requires a little extra planning. Regardless of the feeding position you choose, you will probably need some extra pillows or large cushions. Some mothers find special pillows designed especially for feeding twins to be useful. There are a variety of these on the market. The Australian Multiple Birth Association may be able to give you more information about these and other helpful resources.

As you get ready to feed, lie your babies safely on the bed or on the floor beside you where you can reach them without having to get up, or place them at each end of the couch, safely wedged between a pillow and the armrest. When you are comfortably seated, place a pillow across your lap and either raise your feet on a stool or put a pillow under your knees so that your back is straight and supported and you are not leaning forward over the babies.

There are several different ways you can position your twins for feeding, including the classic twin hold (often also called the football or underarm hold), the parallel hold, the criss-cross hold and the front 'v' hold. If you are beginning to feel like a ruck rover in training, take heart. Each position is really quite simple. It's just that telling you about

*Underarm hold*

it rather than showing you, makes it seem more complicated. If you study the pictures of each hold you will see that it is really a matter of common sense. The one that suits you best will depend on the ages and stages of your babies.

### Twin, football or underarm hold

This is one of the most popular positions as it is the easiest to use when you don't have anyone around to help you. It is probably the most practical position for small babies, leaving two hands free, and puts no pressure on your abdomen if you have had a caesarean delivery. Lie your babies with their feet facing backwards and tucked under your arms and their faces towards yours. Support your babies with your palms behind their shoulders and with your fingers to guide their heads, and lift them to your breasts (one baby at a time while they need help attaching). Use your elbows to hug your babies to you. Raise your knees high enough to ensure that a pillow on your lap will support the babies' heads at your breasts without you having to lean over uncomfortably. This will leave your hands free.

*Photograph by Lesley McBurney*

*Parallel hold*

## Parallel hold

This is less conspicuous but more difficult when your babies are young. When your babies are older, you can feed like this without pillows, as one baby's body will support the head of the other. This makes it more convenient when you are feeding away from home. Hold the first baby in the normal nursing position (across your lap). Lie the second baby gently on the body of, and parallel to, the first baby, so that her head is at your other breast and supported with your hand behind her shoulders. Both babies will be lying in the same direction. Raise your knees to support your arms as you hold your babies.

*Front 'v' hold*

*Photograph by Lesley McBurney*

## Front 'v' hold

This is a good method for feeding at night and helpful if you cannot sit comfortably after delivery. It may be difficult with tiny babies, as you will have limited control over their heads. Support your back so that you can sit comfortably semi-reclined. Place a baby at each breast so they are facing each other and their knees are bent and touching. Support their backs with your arms while your hands cup their bottoms.

## Criss-cross hold

This is easier after about six weeks when your babies are bigger, sucking more strongly, and can attach more easily and securely. Make sure your elbows and back are well supported with pillows. Place the heaviest baby in the normal nursing position. Gently lie the second baby across the first so they are criss-crossed, facing each other, each at one breast. Support their backs with your arms and clasp your hands under their bottoms when you need to bring them close to you.

## When it seems two much

Having twins can be twice as tiring as well as twice as exciting, and the extra demands can place a lot of stress on your family. Trying to find time for yourselves as a couple, as well as for any other children you may have, let alone time for yourselves as individuals, may sometimes seem impossible. That is why it is important to be realistic about what you can and cannot do. Stick to the bare essentials when it comes to household tasks and accept the help of anyone who offers, such as friends, relatives or your local Australian Breastfeeding Association group. You may like to join the Australian Multiple Birth Association, which can offer practical as well as moral support, including the hiring of equipment. Only those who are the parents of twins themselves will probably ever understand. That's why it will be helpful to share your feelings with others with twins.

There are likely to be times when you think that it is all just too difficult and wonder if your problems may be related to breastfeeding. It is more likely that any problems are due to the demands of two babies and the exhaustion that follows. Mixing infant formula and disinfecting bottles is hard work, and twice as time-consuming for twins. Rather than resort to bottle-feeding, you may find it more practical and helpful to get the extra support that you need (either moral or practical or both) so that you can continue to breastfeed, which will be far more convenient for you and the family in the long run.

# The sick or disabled child

The shock and distress of discovering that your baby is sick or disabled can blow your dreams of parenthood out of the water as you struggle with your fears about your baby's survival.

If your baby's illness or disability means he must be separated from you soon after birth, or for lengthy periods in a humidicrib or to undergo surgery, you and your partner will naturally feel anxious and helpless as you watch 'experts' take over, and instead of holding and feeding your baby at your breast as you planned, you may be sitting alone with a breast pump, feeling miserable.

*breastfeeding your baby is a major contribution to his wellbeing*

*Photograph by Lesley McBurney*

*Above: Baby with Down syndrome*

*Below: Baby with a cleft lip and palate*

*Photograph by Leanne Webb*

Finding out as much as possible about your baby's illness or disability, by talking to your medical adviser or other parents or support groups, may help ease your distress. However, by breastfeeding your baby, you will be making a major contribution to his wellbeing and giving him the comfort and love that he especially needs. The nutritive and disease-preventing properties of breastmilk are even more vital for premature and sick babies and those with health-threatening disabilities.

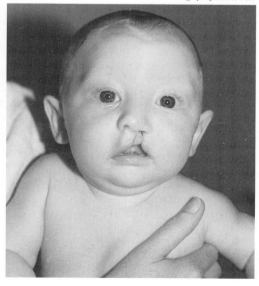

Breastfeeding a baby who is sick or has a disability is not always easy, especially if your baby continues to stay in hospital long after you are sent home. You will need to learn to express and store your milk to establish and maintain your supply. Remember that by keeping up your supply, you are doing the best for your baby. As he grows stronger, you will be able to put him to the breast (unless he has a physical condition that means he will have to rely on expressed breastmilk alone) and enjoy breastfeeding under more normal and relaxing circumstances.

*Expressing for my babies allowed me to feel like their mother. Every other aspect of their care was done by the hospital. Breastmilk was the only thing I could do for them as a mother.*

As often as you need to, talk to your Australian Breastfeeding Association counsellor and others who can support you. The association has a number of helpful, practical booklets on breastfeeding babies with conditions such as Down syndrome, clefts of the lip and/or palate and a guide to breastfeeding and hospitalisation.

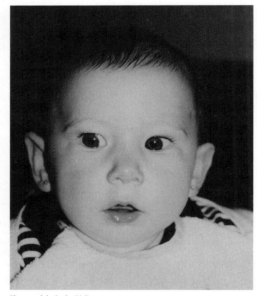

*Photograph by Lesley McBurney*

*Baby born with Pierre Robin syndrome (small chin and cleft palate)*

## CHAPTER EIGHT

# Looking after yourself

Photograph by Susan D'Arcy

*You will need time to get used to the idea of being a mother, to get to know your baby and to bounce back physically.*

- How life changes with a new baby
- Looking after yourself with regard to diet, exercise and smoking
- How alcohol and medications fit in with breastfeeding
- Concerns about pesticides in breastmilk
- Taking time out for yourself

*Photograph by Vicki Bell*

Throughout your pregnancy, especially if this is your first baby, you probably felt very special. Your partner, family, friends, and even strangers may have constantly asked about your health, your feelings and plans. When your baby finally arrived though, the focus of attention understandably, moved to her.

Now it probably seems there is no-one more important in the world — or your world at least — than your baby. The emotional and physical commitment she requires from you may leave you little time to care for yourself.

However, caring for yourself is important too. If you are exhausted and run-down, you will be less able to cope with day-to-day tasks. Feeling lousy will also affect your relationships with your partner and your baby, as you will not be able to enjoy this precious time. Learning to breastfeed and to care for your new baby, as well as care for yourself, your home and any other children you may have, on far less sleep than you may be used to, seems like a lot to expect of anyone, but amazingly new mothers are expected to take it in their stride.

## The new you

Everyone tells you that things change after you have a baby; that you will have less time for other activities, and particularly less time for yourself, but most new parents don't really believe that much will change. You may even have anticipated this as 'time-off' from paid work, and have planned to do lots of gardening and maybe take on some study. In some ways you are right. This will certainly be a learning phase. Babies have a way of teaching their parents and the first lesson is usually that baby comes first.

The second lesson is that managing everything will be a lot easier if you also look after yourself and this may mean asking for help if you need it.

*all babies are very time-consuming and mothering is a 24-hour job*

In the first few days or weeks, you may sometimes find it difficult to even get out of your dressing gown before lunch. Rest assured that there are hundreds of other mothers living nearby who are probably in the same boat. Babies are very time-consuming and mothering, unlike paid work, is a 24-hour job. You will need time to get used to the idea of being a mother, to get to know your baby and to bounce back physically.

If you are awaiting the birth of your baby, particularly if you are feeling that 'nesting' instinct coming on, now is the time to cook and freeze meals in preparation for those first, busy weeks at home with your baby. It's also the best time to accept practical help from those who offer it.

Mobiles and bunny rugs are lovely gifts, but some home help will be far more useful to a new mother. So too will the gift of a nappy-wash service for a few weeks or months, or the offer to cook a week's worth of casseroles, or to be available to pick things up from the supermarket when necessary.

### take the offer

Some women feel quite offended at offers of help, as they see it as a presumption that they aren't able to cope. Don't take offence; take the offer. It is recognition of the fact that you will have a far more important job to do, learning to mother your new baby.

This period of intense need is very brief. It is far better for you to relax and enjoy your new baby than to have a clean and tidy home, and a meal on the table. Of course, the housework still needs to be done. Just try to make sure it is done by somebody else. This is not meant to sound glib. You cannot expect to come home from hospital with a new baby and do everything you did before. If your partner or other family members or friends cannot help at this time, if you can manage it, you may like to consider paid help, or a serious reorganisation of your priorities for the time being.

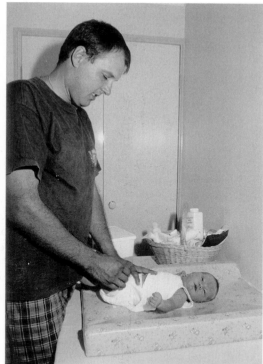

*Photograph by Sylvie Jackson*

## Diet

A healthy and varied diet is important at any time, but particularly when you are pregnant or breastfeeding and catering for the needs of two. This doesn't mean that you must eat for two, just that you must take responsibility for two. While there's a common belief that milk production is influenced by a mother's nutritional status, research in the United Kingdom and Africa found that the ability of poorly-nourished women to produce breastmilk was not greatly different to that of well-nourished mothers.

Nature will ensure that your baby will not miss out on nutrients if you live on cola, chips and chocolate biscuits, as your body will still produce excellent milk — but you will look and feel a lot better if you eat well.

### the return to pre-pregnancy weight varies

Some women lose the fat stores built up during pregnancy quickly and easily after the birth; others find them much more difficult to shake. If you are still a few kilograms overweight, but otherwise healthy and eating a nutritious diet, try not to worry too much about the extra weight until your baby gets a little older. The length of time mothers take to return to pre-pregnancy weight varies widely, but is usually sooner (without dieting) in breastfeeding mothers than in those who bottle-feed. A few mothers find they carry a bit of extra weight the whole time they are breastfeeding and lose it when their baby weans.

*Photograph by Yvette O'Dowd*

Now isn't the time to go on a crash or fad diet. Diets that are not nutritionally-balanced are unsuitable for pregnant and breastfeeding women, and feeling hungry all the time will probably make you irritable and less able to cope.

## Exercise

Exercise is important to your health and your sense of wellbeing. Regular, moderate exercise will give you more energy, a greater sense of wellbeing, help you juggle the demands of being a mother, and protect you against osteoporosis and heart disease later in life.

If you are eating well, have lost weight, but still can't fit into your pre-pregnancy clothes, you may need to tighten and tone a few muscles that have been stretched during pregnancy. This can take time and patience, and may never result in the slim, girlish figure of your youth. Be realistic about what you can achieve and you are more likely to maintain both a good exercise routine and a healthy diet.

You may find the type of exercise that you enjoyed before pregnancy cannot now be done without a babysitter. You may be lucky enough to be able to arrange this by either leaving your baby with your partner, parents or a friend, or hiring a sitter. If you can't, try walking with your baby in a pram (or sling) to the shops, the park, or try an aerobics class at home, courtesy of the local video shop. Many recreation centres hold special classes for mothers, with a crèche provided.

Check with your doctor before beginning a formal exercise program. This is especially important during pregnancy and the first two months after giving birth. Postnatal exercises designed for new mothers help you avoid later problems such as incontinence and

*Photograph by Dianne Griffiths*

prolapse of the uterus, and to regain your pre-pregnancy shape.

Studies on the effects of exercise on milk supply have shown that moderate exercise is fine for breastfeeding mothers. Some women report a decrease in supply after very vigorous exercise. Others feel that it boosts their supply. Feeding your baby before you exercise is a good idea, because your breasts will not be so full and heavy. A good supportive bra, properly fitted, will help you exercise more comfortably and will help ward off blockages. Avoid tight clothes that flatten the breasts. Check your breasts regularly for lumps caused by blockage of the milk ducts, particularly underneath and near the armpits. Be careful not to bump or bruise your breasts. You may find exercises that involve lying on your stomach uncomfortable. Dancing, skipping and bike riding are all effective and enjoyable ways to get exercise with or without your baby. Remember to take a shower afterwards, as some babies don't like the taste of perspiration with their breastmilk.

## Smoking

Research shows that smoking during pregnancy has a number of consequences for babies. The incidence of perinatal mortality (death of an infant just before, during or just after birth) rises sharply if you are a smoker.

Your baby may be an average of 200 grams lighter. The blood flow in the umbilical cord, which carries nutrients to your baby, slows minutes after you start to smoke, and this can last up to an hour. Your baby could be shorter and is more likely to have learning difficulties.

The risk of your baby dying of sudden infant death syndrome (SIDS) is greater. In her first year, your baby has a much higher risk of developing pneumonia or bronchitis. At preschool age your child is likely to spend twice as many days in hospital.

If you smoke during breastfeeding, the chemicals from the cigarettes pass through the milk to your baby. Your child has a greater risk of developing respiratory illnesses and colic and may have long-term health problems caused by passive smoking.

Knowing all this, the question you will have if you are a smoker is: 'Should I breastfeed?' Research generally suggests that if the choice is between smoking and breastfeeding, or smoking and not breastfeeding, then breastfeed. Breastfeeding limits some of the harmful effects of smoking. For those who continue to smoke, smoke less. Smoke soon after a feed. The half-life of nicotine is around 90 minutes, meaning that it rapidly decreases in concentration in breastmilk. Therefore, the longer time between smoking and a feed, the less exposure. Smoke somewhere away from your baby, keeping your house as smoke-free as possible.

*Photograph by Amanda Radovic*

## Alcohol

Alcohol is, of course, a drug that can be passed to your baby via the placenta while you are pregnant and via your breastmilk when you are breastfeeding. The amount a baby receives if you drink it in moderation (one or two standard drinks, only occasionally) is unlikely to harm a healthy baby, although some don't like the taste of breastmilk after their mothers have alcoholic drinks and may even temporarily refuse to feed.

Chronic and binge drinking are problems — high levels of alcohol are believed to significantly suppress milk production and may affect your baby's neurological development. However, if you do like the occasional drink, a few feeds of your breastmilk with a tiny amount of alcohol are still better than artificial milk for your baby. Exposure can be minimised by feeding your baby just before having the drink, and by the time he wants another feed, chances are that the alcohol has been cleared from your body by your liver — perhaps completely — if it has been more than a couple of hours.

If you have had a bigger night out than usual and you've had more drinks than you planned, it's best to wait a few hours until the alcohol is more-or-less out of your system before you breastfeed your baby. You can express and discard the milk if your breasts feel over-full. However, expressing won't speed up the natural expulsion of the alcohol from your system. At any point in time, your milk-alcohol level is about the same as your blood-alcohol level.

## Medications and breastfeeding

During pregnancy and breastfeeding, your baby's health is interlinked to your own, so it's no wonder that many mothers are concerned about taking medications. Exclusive breastfeeding is now recommended for your baby's first six months, with breastmilk remaining his most important food for the first 12 months. In that time, even the healthiest mothers are likely to need to take at least one medication, and some will need treatment for chronic medical conditions.

### most drugs can be used safely by breastfeeding mothers

It's reassuring to know that, with very few exceptions, most drugs can be used safely by breastfeeding mothers. All medications enter breastmilk, but most do so in concentrations so low that there is no effect on the baby. Authorities believe that, if the daily dose transferred to a baby is less than 10 percent of the mother's dose, a medication is safe, unless that drug is completely contraindicated for breastfeeding. Your body provides natural barriers in the cells that create breastmilk, which means that most drugs have difficulty in passing into your milk, so on average, an absolutely minimal percentage of your dose of a medication reaches your baby.

### make an informed choice

Before prescribing any medication for you, your medical adviser should be aware that you are breastfeeding. All drugs are divided into classes, and within each class there will be a number of safe options from which to choose. All prescription drugs are required to go through extensive testing. Medication packaging contains consumer information, which will usually tell you whether this drug is safe during lactation. This information is provided both as a decision-making tool for you and to protect the manufacturer against possible litigation, so is understandably conservative.

Some choices are straightforward, but if your doctor is undecided about whether or not you can safely breastfeed when taking a particular medication, ask that they check with drug information experts. With so many new drugs available, it's often difficult to keep abreast of them all. Fortunately, in Australia we have a number of excellent sources of information available to consumers and health professionals about specific medications and drug interactions. If you have any questions about the medication you have been prescribed, you can have them answered for the cost of a phone call.

### Drug Information Centres

NATIONAL: Medicines Line: 1300 888 763 9.00 am – 6.00 pm AEST (for mothers)
Therapeutic Advice and Information Service (TAIS): 1300 138 677 (for health professionals only)

| | | |
|---|---|---|
| ACT/NSW | (02) 9382 6539 | Mothersafe Medications in Pregnancy and Lactation Service (Sydney metropolitan) Mon–Fri |
| ACT/NSW | 1800 647 848 | Mothersafe Medications in Pregnancy and Lactation Service (Non-metropolitan) Mon–Fri |
| SA | (08) 8161 7222 | Women's and Children's Hospital |
| VIC | (03) 9594 2361 | Monash Medical Centre Mon–Fri 8.45 am – 5.15 pm |
| VIC | (03) 9344 2277 | Royal Women's Hospital 8.15 am – 5.30 pm |
| WA | (08) 9340 2723 | King Edward Memorial Hospital for Women Mon–Fri 8.30 am – 5.00 pm |
| TAS | 1300 888 763 | Medicines Line (National number) |
| QLD | 1300 888 763 | Medicines Line (National number) |

### Internet resources

http://www.perinatology.com/exposures/druglist.htm
http://neonatal.ttuhsc.edu/lact/ (forum for questions from health professionals, but anyone can use the site as a guest: http://neonatal.ama.ttuhsc.edu/cgi-bin/discus/discus.cgi)
http://www.nlm.nih.gov/medlineplus/druginformation.html

All details up to date at time of printing.

## safe options for common conditions

Most of us are struck down with some sort of a virus at least once a year. There is a variety of non-sedating antihistamines, nasal sprays and analgesics from which to safely choose. Most antibiotics are suitable for breastfeeding mothers. Some antibiotics may cause your baby to be a little unsettled or have temporary diarrhoea, but these are fairly insignificant compared to the importance of combating an infection.

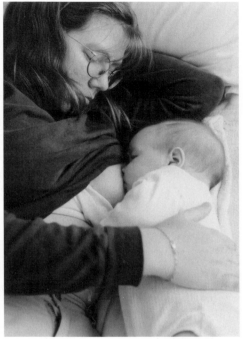

Penicillins, for example, enter breastmilk at very low levels and have not been shown to produce side effects in babies. However, medications that contain pseudoephedrine may reduce your breastmilk supply. Drugs that are sedating can predispose your baby to breathing difficulties as well as affecting his sleep, so you will need to talk to your doctor about the best options if you need to take cold or allergy preparations or analgesics.

Some other drugs have the potential to affect your supply, either positively or negatively. For instance, drugs that stimulate prolactin (the

*Photograph by Susan D'Arcy*

hormone that is involved in the production of breastmilk) can increase milk production, whereas drugs that contain oestrogen (such as some contraceptives) have been shown to reduce supply.

Given that about 15–20 percent of women experience some level of postnatal depression, it's reassuring to know that there are antidepressants that are considered safe during lactation, even though there are others that may need to be more closely monitored by your doctor for any side effects.

There are a few special situations in which it may be necessary for a mother to express and discard her breastmilk; for instance if she is taking radioactive drugs, certain anti-cancer drugs or if she is using drugs of abuse. If she is able to maintain her supply until the drug is out of her system, she will be able to resume breastfeeding.

## over-the-counter remedies and herbal preparations

Before you take over-the-counter preparations from your health food shop or pharmacy, you should also check that they are safe. While we often assume that herbal remedies are harmless, this is not always

*Photograph by Susan D'Arcy*

true. Keep in mind that herbal preparations are not required to have the same level of testing and proof of efficacy as prescription drugs, so we know less about their side effects during lactation. From what we do know, some are considered to be quite safe while some have been shown to contain components that are unsafe. For instance, some herbal teas, such as peppermint, raspberry and rose hip, are considered safe during lactation, while herbs such as comfrey and sassafras are not recommended. It's a good idea to do your homework before you take particular herbs, especially if you are taking them in conjunction with prescription medicines.

*breastfeed just before you take medications*

Ideally, you should breastfeed your baby just before you take any medication. This will mean that by the next time you feed her the level of the drug in your bloodstream will be much lower. Most drugs are absorbed into your bloodstream, rise to a peak and then decline. The faster they decline, the better for breastfed babies. Drugs whose levels decline quickly are said to have short half-lives. You should be cautious about sustained-release medications (drugs with long half-lives) and any drugs that have several active components, although they are usually still safe. It is likely that you will still be able to take them if they're the best choice to treat your condition, but your doctor may ask you to watch for any effects on your baby.

There are some general principles that apply when taking any medications while you are breastfeeding:

○ Take medications only when they are necessary, and when the benefits outweigh the risks.
○ Choose medications that have been clearly proven to be the best option for breastfeeding mothers.
○ Choose preparations that are non-sedating and are low in toxicity.
○ If possible, avoid sustained-release medications that stay longer in your body.
○ Take the medication just after a breastfeed.
○ If possible, choose medications that act locally, eg a topical ointment rather than tablets.

## Pesticides

From time to time, you may read a newspaper article or hear a radio report about the levels of pesticides found in breastmilk. Although this may sound alarming, breastfeeding is still recommended. A build-up of organochlorides — such as dieldrin, aldrin, chlordane and other related compounds — are found in body fat, in various foods and in animals. Breastmilk is sometimes used in testing because it is the only convenient, non-invasive method of measuring levels of pesticides that accumulate in body fats in a particular population. These residues are accumulated in all of us simply as a result of living in our environment and are not confined to breastfeeding women.

Weaning your baby from the breast to a bottle will not protect him from contaminants in the environment. Artificial milks can be high in aluminium and radioactive substances and heavy metals tend to accumulate more in the milks of grazing animals. There is no evidence that any of the levels found in breastmilk in Australia pose any danger whatever to babies. In fact the opposite has been found — that the breastfed babies in areas of the world with relatively high contamination levels had better outcomes than those who were infant-formula-fed. Levels have, in fact, dropped fairly dramatically in the past couple of decades, but some of the things you can do to reduce any possible build-up of pesticides in your body fat and that of your family are avoid having your house treated with insecticides, and eat a wide range of foods, preferably peeled but at least well-washed.

## Taking time out

One of the rarest commodities a mother can have is time just for herself. Even the most private acts, such as going to the toilet, become public as toddlers are fascinated by, and like to be included in, absolutely everything their parents do. Try to set aside a little personal time for yourself right from the start.

After giving birth you may feel a little bedraggled. Your hair and skin, which glowed in the middle trimester of pregnancy, may have

*Photograph by Yvette O'Dowd*

dulled due to changed hormone levels, your tummy may feel flabby and you will probably feel less than glamorous.

You may feel better if you can find the time to have your hair done, have a facial or a massage — anything where you can be pampered for a change. Or perhaps you are just longing for an uninterrupted phone conversation, a bubble bath, a yoga class or a coffee or some social contact with someone who knew you before you were a mother.

If you are happy to leave your baby, but money is short for babysitters, perhaps you could arrange a contra deal with another mother. Or better still, your partner can have some precious time with his baby on a weekend or evening while you do something for yourself.

Photograph by Amanda Radovic

Sometimes you may not want to actually *do* anything. You may simply want to have the house or the bed to yourself for a few hours. You can express milk if you will miss a feed time, and while it may seem like a lot of trouble to organise for someone else to care for your baby for even a few hours, it may be worth it. This time out will help you to relax and feel cared for and energised.

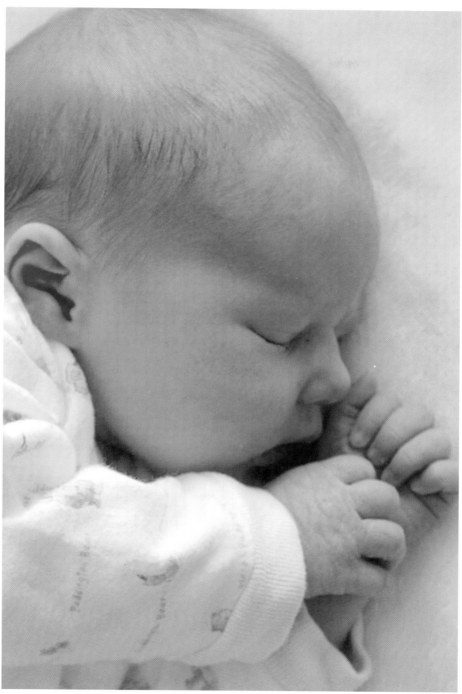

Photograph by Prue Carr

*A baby blissed out on your breastmilk gives you a great sense of achievement*

Photograph by Dane Carter

*A breastfed baby is a joyful addition to any celebration*

Photograph by Davina Hurst

*Breastfeeding creates a loving bond between you and your baby*

Photograph by Shannon Bellette

*A breastfeed provides a welcome break in your busy day*

## CHAPTER NINE

# Sex and breastfeeding

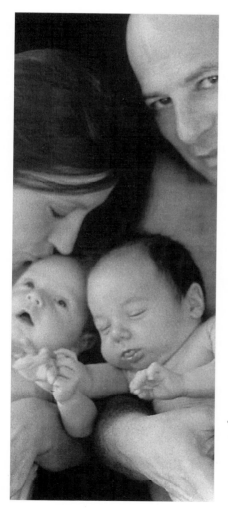

- *Physiological factors related to both the birth and breastfeeding*
- *Psychological factors*
- *Contraception*
- *Getting your sex-life back*

*Don't expect too much of yourselves and be reassured that your sex life will resume, in one form or another, eventually.*

Photograph by Susan D'Arcy

For some new mothers, this very title is a contradiction in terms. Many couples find that becoming parents puts extra tensions on their relationship. Even before becoming parents, we were all affected by tiredness, other commitments, tensions in our relationships, and of course, hormones. Add a new baby, and all the extra work this entails, and you may wonder how any couple ever manages to have a second child. The fact that there are so many families with two, three or more children is proof that lack of interest in, or opportunity for, sex after the birth of a baby is usually temporary.

Talk to your partner about your feelings and ask about his. It is natural to have fears and questions about making love after the birth of your baby. It is also natural for patterns of lovemaking to remain disrupted for some time. Some couples don't enjoy intercourse for at least two months after the birth, and sometimes much longer, depending on the amount of healing needed after the birth. Even by the baby's first birthday, many couples find they are making love less often than they did before the pregnancy.

### babies seem to know when romance is in the air

If you have had a vaginal tear or stitches after the birth due to an episiotomy, or other damage to the vagina, you may be experiencing pain, which will naturally dampen any sexual desire. You may find that your vagina is very dry and intercourse is no longer pleasurable. It is also difficult to relax and enjoy lovemaking knowing that the climax is likely to be a crescendo of screams from the bassinette. Babies seem to know when romance is in the air. Perhaps it is part of their survival mechanism — an ancient instinct to prevent the possibility of any sibling rivals on the scene too soon!

You may find though, that it is breastfeeding, rather than motherhood that is blamed for your lack of libido. Some people still believe that breastfeeding is 'draining' on the mother, or that the intense intimacy

a breastfeeding mother shares with her child displaces the need for intimacy with her partner. This is both true and false. Studies comparing the sexual behaviour of breastfeeding women with women who are not breastfeeding vary in their conclusions. Some say there is no difference, others say breastfeeding women are more sexually active, and still others say the opposite.

## Physiological factors related to the birth

They say that sex is all in the head — that is, your mental attitude has more to do with your sexual feelings than anything else. However, there are several physiological reasons why you may feel less interested in making love right now.

Firstly, for up to six weeks after the birth you will have a vaginal discharge (lochia), and this puts some people off sexual intercourse. (But as long as your doctor has not advised against it, there is no reason you cannot still have intercourse.) Secondly, you are probably exhausted. Tiredness is the most common cause of abstinence in the first weeks or months. Thirdly, you may not be feeling 'sexy'.

Changes in body shape can also affect your feelings about your sexuality. Your breasts, hips and thighs are probably bigger than before. Some spreading and fanning of the outer part of your vagina after the birth is normal, too. The lips of your vagina (labia) may also seem larger and hang down further.

Less obvious will be the change in the strength of your abdominal muscles and your pelvic floor (the region of your anal, vaginal and urinary openings). Weak stomach muscles will prevent you from fitting into your favourite figure-hugging clothes and may lead to some alarming jokes about whether you are still pregnant. This can be rectified by attention to diet and exercise. But weak pelvic floor muscles are no laughing matter, especially if they cause you to wet your pants when you laugh or cough. As you get older, weak pelvic floor muscles can also cause uterine prolapse. You will enjoy sex more and be more easily aroused, and reach orgasm more often and more easily if your pelvic floor muscles are strong, so now's the time to start doing those invisible push-ups.

## Physiological factors related to breastfeeding

As women, rightly or wrongly, we are all used to having our moods blamed on our hormones. During pregnancy, the levels of two reproductive hormones, oestrogen and progesterone, rise and then fall rapidly after birth. Women who do not breastfeed return to their 'normal' hormone levels, ovulate (produce an egg) and menstruate within about three months. However, breastfeeding women generally do not regain pre-pregnancy hormone levels, ovulation or periods until much later.

This delayed fertility is caused by hormones related to breastfeeding indirectly suppressing the release of oestrogen and progesterone. How long this lasts varies from mother to mother. In rare situations, some

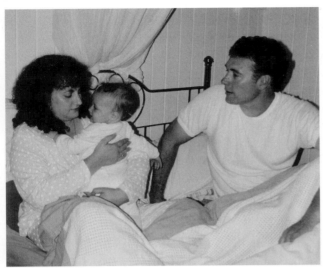

*Photograph by Lesley McBurney*

breastfeeding women become fertile four weeks after delivery and a few can conceive within 12 weeks of giving birth; but for most women, ovulation occurs much later. There are wide variations in the length of postpartum amenorrhoea (no periods), but it is agreed that a woman has 98 percent protection from pregnancy in the first six months after birth, provided she remains amenorrhoeic and her baby is exclusively breastfed.

Low oestrogen levels are generally thought to cause the vaginal wall to become thinner and less elastic and to reduce lubrication. Many mothers find they need to use a lubricant for a while after birth, when having sex.

Having full or leaking breasts can also be uncomfortable or off-putting during intercourse for some people, while others find it a real turn-on. It is common for milk to leak from the breasts during arousal; so is experiencing some sexual arousal while your baby breastfeeds. The reason for this is that the same hormone — oxytocin — triggers both the let-down reflex and orgasm. There is no need to worry about this. Any good feelings that encourage breastfeeding are to a baby's advantage.

## Psychological factors

As if pain, fatigue and hormones were not enough to make you take a detour on the road to sexual fulfilment, there is a positive minefield of emotional problems also set to waylay you. First of all there's fear, of pain, pregnancy; jealousy, of your baby, your partner whose body or lifestyle has not changed as drastically, of others who seem to be coping better; protectiveness of the baby and reluctance to share yourself further; anticlimax, the big event is over as far as you're concerned; disappointment, with the baby, the birth, yourself, your partner; guilty for not instantly loving your baby, for yelling at your toddler again, about not feeling sexy or giving time to your partner; anxiety, over money, not coping, health problems, about not being a good mother and not getting enough sleep; resentment over the constant demands placed on you and your body so that you feel completely 'touched-out'; sadness over the loss of your previous relationship with your partner, your work friends, your old life, control and freedom; boredom, spending too much time at home, feeling trapped; thinking about your own childhood; feeling depressed because of all or some of the above.

Despite all these obstacles, the human body (and the human spirit) is a wonderful thing and happily for most of us, sex usually sprints (or limps) up to the top of our 'to do' list before too long.

## Contraception

The most widely-used oral contraceptives for breastfeeding mothers are the progesterone-only ones (the mini pill, progesterone-only injections and implants). The other most common methods are the intrauterine device (IUD), the diaphragm, condoms, spermicides, and ovulation awareness methods, such as the Billings Method. The combined oral contraceptive is not recommended for breastfeeding mothers. It has been shown to deplete milk supply because it contains oestrogen. It is best to consult your medical adviser about any oral or injected forms of contraception. A family planning doctor will be able to help you decide what is best for you, and will tell you all you need to know about natural planning methods and the use of aids or medication.

## Planning for sex

People often explain their first sexual encounter using the words 'It just happened.' Well, once you become parents, sex seldom 'just happens'

*Photograph by Susan D'Arcy*

unless you plan for it. This might mean planning to make love at 7 pm, just after the baby falls asleep, rather than sitting up watching television and falling into bed at 11 pm, when the baby is likely to wake. It might mean having a passionate picnic on the bed at home while a neighbour or grandparent looks after the baby for an hour. It might mean setting up your toddler and older child with a video and some munchies while you and your partner have a shower together. Remember how creative you had to be when you were courting and had nowhere private to kiss and cuddle? Well, now is a good time to revive some of those exciting, if furtive, times again — even if the back seat of the car is now crowded with capsules and baby seats.

## Talking about it

Let your partner know how you feel, physically and emotionally. If your breasts are sore, or your vagina is dry, tell him. If you don't feel like sex, but would love a cuddle, tell him. If you have had a good night's rest and found yourself fantasising about him while you were doing the dishes, tell him that too. If watching a romantic movie made you feel sexy, tell him that. Even if you don't have intercourse, it will help both of you to realise that you are still sexual people and that there are many ways of relating sexually. Loving each other does not have to be restricted to making love. Touching, bathing together, or those three important words, 'I love you,' are sometimes all that is needed to create intimacy.

Take your time, don't expect too much of yourselves and be reassured that your sex life will resume, in one form or another, eventually. However, this does presume a certain mutual understanding and acceptance. Some partners find lack of interest in sex extremely difficult to accept. If you or your partner is out of balance regarding sex and you are both feeling angry and resentful, you might think about seeking professional help.

Photograph by Amanda Radovic

CHAPTER TEN

# Out and about with your breastfed baby

- *Breastfeeding away from home*
- *Coping with criticism*
- *Your rights*
- *Travelling with your breastfed baby*

*A breastfeeding mother does not necessarily need to leave her baby to have her freedom.*

Photograph by Prue Carr

*Photograph by Des Murad*

One of the 'virtues' attributed to bottle-feeding is that it gives a mother freedom, because it allows her to leave her baby to be fed by someone else. A breastfeeding mother does not necessarily need to leave her baby to have her freedom. She can take her baby with her anywhere and breastfeed him anytime, without having to worry about whether she has disinfected bottles, measured formula powder, has access to clean water and bottle-warming facilities, or has briefed a babysitter. So make the most of the flexibility of breastfeeding and enjoy showing off your beautiful new baby.

Every day, thousands of mothers breastfeed while they are out and about with their babies — breastfeeding is simply a normal and natural part of their day.

## Getting out of the house

When you're used to just picking up your handbag and car keys and shutting the door behind you, going out with a new baby can seem a bit daunting at first. It needn't take military precision, but a bit of planning can mean you at least make it to the shops before they shut.

Don't try to get the house tidied and the washing on the line — by the time you've done that you might be too tired to bother going out. It will still be there waiting for you when you get home and you might feel more like tackling it after some time out. Life with a new baby can feel a bit isolating. Sometimes a trip to the shops or to the park, where you can catch up on what's happening outside your own cocoon, can give you a new burst of energy.

### just go!

Ignore the phone for the last 15 minutes before you leave. Unless you're expecting an important call, any others can wait until you return.

Nappies and other essentials can be packed ahead of time so that you just have to pick up the bag and go. If you're really organised, you might have a bag of baby supplies that you keep stocked and ready for outings. The great thing about a breastfed baby is that you can travel light!

Think about what you'll wear. Separates are ideal for ease of breastfeeding. Tops that lift up can help you feel more confident than having to completely unbutton. If your bra can be easily opened using one hand, you will be able to put your baby to the breast with the minimum of fuss. Some mothers like to take a lightweight bunny rug to shield their breastfeeding baby, particularly if the baby is easily distracted by what's happening nearby.

## Anywhere, anytime

All you and your baby need is somewhere to sit. That might mean in a shopping centre, a coffee shop, on the bus or train or in a park — anywhere you want to go.

Photograph by Dez Murad

You don't have to ask for permission. You have the right to breastfeed wherever and whenever your baby needs to be fed. Sadly, because no story involving breastfeeding is more likely to make the headlines than one about a mother being discriminated against for breastfeeding her baby in a public place, it's not surprising that many women feel uncertain about meeting their babies' needs.

### don't be put off

Breastfeeding is not only important to your baby and to you, it's important to the whole community. No mother should be expected to feed her baby in the ladies' rest room. No-one would dream of eating their own lunch in the toilets, yet some people think it's acceptable for babies. In the unlikely event that someone 'politely' points you in that direction, equally politely point out that anti-discrimination legislation is on your side and you don't have to hide away to breastfeed. It's just one part of a mother's day, not a slightly embarrassing secret.

Eating out is more than sharing food. If you're out with your partner or meeting friends to share a meal, you will want to do just that, not be off feeding your baby, no matter how luxurious a baby care room may be. You might prefer a corner table where you can sit with your back to other diners, or you might prefer to sit at a table outside watching the world go by. Just do what feels comfortable to you. If you have other children, feeding somewhere separate is impossible. You'll be helping baby attach to the breast with one hand and making sure your kinder kid doesn't spill that milkshake with the other.

*it's ok to feel a bit shy at first*

In the early days, while you and your baby are still learning to breastfeed, feed times can be a little awkward. You might feel more comfortable feeding somewhere where you can concentrate on getting it right. If you prefer to breastfeed in a baby care room, you might be lucky enough to have an Australian Breastfeeding Association approved facility near you. Supported by *Australian Parents* magazine, these rooms provide privacy and comfortable seating, hot and cold water and hand-drying facilities, somewhere clean and safe to change nappies with hygienic waste disposal — all in a smoke-free environment. For your nearest Australian Breastfeeding Association Baby Care Room, check the association's website: http://www.breastfeeding.asn.au. Alternatively, look for the association's Breastfeeding Welcome Here sticker (at left). These breastfeeding-friendly businesses are endorsed because of their welcoming attitude from staff and management, their smoke-free environment and space for a pram.

Be prepared for compliments. The sight of a baby peacefully breastfeeding brings out the best in all of us. You might be surprised by a smile from a stranger or an encouraging word. Smile back and accept the compliment!

**Breastfeeding welcome here**

Australian Breastfeeding Association

## Coping with criticism

If you do receive criticism for breastfeeding your baby in a public place, don't be intimidated, be outraged. It gets much better results.

One reason for some people's discomfit at seeing a woman breastfeeding in public may be that it is a new experience for them. In Australia, we lead largely segregated lives. Although people now recognise that there are many types of family other than the nuclear family, it is still rare to find generations of families living together under the one roof. This means young people growing up are not often directly exposed to the norms of life and death, including birth and breastfeeding. This may explain why seeing a mother breastfeed her baby in public is so confronting for some people.

While it's probably assumed that most criticism would come from men, it has been the experience of mothers who have contacted the Australian Breastfeeding Association that negative comments are more likely to come from other women. Perhaps the sight of another woman breastfeeding touches deep-seated emotions and beliefs about the complainant's own infant feeding experience and what is appropriate behaviour. Where comments have come from men, it more often involves mothers being asked to move to a private breastfeeding area in the (usually misguided) belief that she will feel more comfortable. So, while on the face of it, we would assume that it's the actual sight of a breast that some people find confronting, this seems to be a less important factor.

When the person breastfeeding her child is also a public figure, people feel more entitled to express strong views, as there is a perception that a public figure is public property, especially one that is on the public payroll, such as a politician. In our culture, work and family life are also very separate. There is also the perception that a mother's time during working hours belongs to the employer, not the baby. This may explain the outrage that resulted when a newly-elected Member of Parliament breastfed her 11-day-old daughter in the chamber of the Victorian Legislative Assembly. One woman writing to the media about the issue, mirroring the view of others said: 'She needs to make a choice. Be a mum or an MP. Some jobs are conducive to juggling careers with motherhood, but being an MP is not one of them.'

### breastfeeding as a simple, natural, womanly function

Fortunately, with most women breastfeeding their babies and more people recognising breastfeeding as a simple, natural, womanly

*Photograph by Des Murad*

function, attitudes are changing. Controversies like this, although seemingly negative at the time, often have positive outcomes. The incident galvanised this MP to campaign for better facilities for parents generally. Legislative rules were later changed to allow babies to be breastfed in the chamber and the right of hungry babies to be fed in public places was firmly placed back on the public agenda.

## Your rights

Controversy over breastfeeding in some public places may imply that breastfeeding is unnatural, undesirable or even illegal. Nothing could be further from the truth. Don't forget that conflict and bad news is more likely to make the newspapers, radio and television. Conflict is the essence of news reporting. The fact that things are going along swimmingly is simply not news. That's why you don't hear much about the many mothers who happily breastfeed at work, in shopping centres, in parks, in restaurants, in railway carriages or just about anywhere, without raising an eyebrow, let alone a ruckus.

In fact, breastfeeding in Australia is a right, not a privilege. In October 2002, the Australian Government amended the Sex Discrimination Act 1984 to explicitly recognise breastfeeding as a potential ground for unlawful discrimination. The Act had always protected the rights of breastfeeding mothers, but did not specifically mention breastfeeding. The amendment aimed to address any confusion. The Act makes sex discrimination against the law and gives effect to Australia's international obligations under the Convention on the Elimination of All Forms of Discrimination Against Women (CEDAW).

Photograph by Yvette O'Dowd

In addition, several individual states have enacted their own laws to protect the rights of breastfeeding women in areas such as work, education, and the provision of goods and services. Details vary from state to state so check your local agency or the Human Rights and Equal Opportunity Commission's website for details. If you feel you have grounds for complaint, you can contact the commission on 1300 656 419 or online. Another useful publication is *Getting to Know the Sex Discrimination Act: A Guide for Young Women*. The guide includes all you need to know about your rights and responsibilities and is available online or from the Human Rights Commission.

*the law protects your baby's right to be breastfed*

As the former federal Sex Discrimination Commissioner, Susan Halliday, stated: 'Common sense dictates that hungry babies be fed and Australian parents have the right to choose the option of breastfeeding their children. For many years it has been illegal under federal, state and territory law to discriminate against breastfeeding women in the provision of goods and services, including service at restaurants, clubs, pubs and theatres and on public transport. It will be a particularly sad day when, in Australia, a woman is penalised for properly caring for her child in a public place.'

## Travelling with your breastfed baby

Breastfeeding gives your baby a distinct advantage while you are travelling. His meals are always available, at just the right temperature and are not affected by the climate or surrounding environment, or any problems with hygiene. Travelling as a family can be exhausting, as well as exhilarating, so not having to worry about your baby's meals is a big bonus. It also saves money.

If you are travelling overseas and need to be vaccinated yourself, or to take preventative medications, make sure you tell your doctor that you are breastfeeding and discuss any effects these medications may have on your baby. You will also need to discuss any special protection that your baby may need, although your breastmilk will be an important aid in boosting his immune system.

*Photograph by Brooke Randell*

When you are travelling by plane, it will be more comfortable for your baby if he feeds during take-off and landing when the air pressure changes inside the plane. If he is unsettled by the changed environment and being on the go, your breasts will provide important familiar comfort. If you are travelling somewhere hot, make sure that you drink plenty of fluids as your baby may be thirstier and you do not want to risk becoming dehydrated yourself.

*it's a good idea to plan ahead*

Airports and train stations usually have a parents' room, if you would like to feed in private or to change a nappy. If possible, it's a good idea to plan ahead. Try to find out what facilities are available for you and your baby before you embark on your trip.

If you are travelling by car, never feed your baby while the car is moving. This would involve one or both of you being unrestrained and is extremely dangerous and illegal. It is much safer and more pleasant to stop and have a bite to eat or a drink yourself while you feed your baby, perhaps at a roadside stop or picnic spot. It may be a good idea to carry an umbrella for shade as well as rain, plenty of extra drinks for you and plenty of extra nappies, cloths for wiping and changes of clothes. Car air conditioners can sometimes cause dehydration, so your baby may need extra feeds. If your car has no air conditioning, your baby can get quite hot in the back seat. Try to ensure he is always shaded from the back and side windows and offer him frequent feeds.

*Photograph by Dianne Griffiths*

CHAPTER ELEVEN

# Asleep and awake

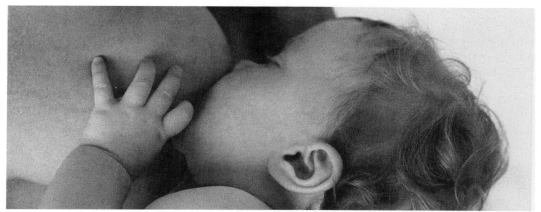

*Photograph by Lou Slater*

*It's healthy and normal for babies and young children to wake during the night and to need the attention and security of their parents.*

- *Babies' sleep — what's normal*
- *Getting your baby to sleep*
- *Reasons for night waking*
- *What's wrong with 'controlled' crying*
- *How to co-sleep safely with your baby*

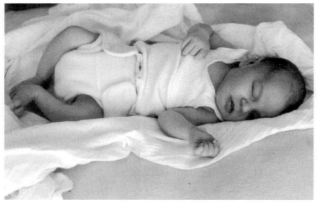

*Photograph by Susan D'Arcy*

Sleeping, or more correctly the lack of it, is a big issue for most parents. Perhaps this is because in our culture, babies are still expected to fit in with adults rather than the other way round. The notion that a 'good' baby is one that is undemanding also affects parents' and society's expectations.

## Sleeping like a baby

For some babies, sleep, long and sound, comes early, but this is very rare. While all babies sleep, most take quite a while to turn it into a habit, that is, something done at regular and predictable times and for lengthy periods.

Soon after you return home, most people who ask after the baby will ask: 'Is he sleeping through?' Having to confess that your baby wakes frequently, even after he's reached the age when you were told he would 'settle into routine', may make you feel guilty, embarrassed, frustrated or apologetic. Once you realise that the definition of sleeping through in a baby is five hours, not the eight hours we associate with a good night's sleep in adults, your expectations of your baby may change.

Babies' sleeping habits change as they mature. Today's good sleeper may be tomorrow's teething and tossing baby. Remember too that a baby's sleep patterns are different from an adult's.

There are two basic types of sleep — quiet sleep, when the breathing is slow and regular and the body hardly moves, and active sleep. Very young babies usually sleep a lot as they need to conserve energy to grow, but about 60 percent of this is Rapid Eye Movement (REM) sleep, the more active sleep, when breathing is faster and more irregular and there are lots of body and facial movements. New babies spend about twice as much time as adults in active sleep, and it's thought that frequent arousals may play a part in protecting a baby against SIDS.

As your baby grows, the proportion of quiet sleep gradually increases to about 80 percent of sleep time and REM sleep decreases to 20 percent, as the brain matures. Large amounts of REM may provide the brain with extra stimulation to help it develop. These two types of sleep alternate to form a cycle. One cycle of quiet and REM sleep takes about 90 minutes in adults but is much shorter in babies and children.

*your baby's sleep patterns do not match yours*

The issue may be that your baby's sleep patterns do not match yours. In our society, a baby over the age of three months or so seems to be expected to develop a regular sleep/wake pattern that fits in with our lifestyle. However, this is usually not realistic and brings stresses of its own when our baby appears not to 'measure up'.

It's healthy and normal for babies and young children to wake during the night and to need the attention and security of their parents. Babies are more likely to develop secure attachments if their emotional needs are met. Sometimes it is a matter of coming to terms with the reality of babies compared to the fantasy. If other people's expectations and opinions are making you feel pressured, a little white lie may be in order. Just nod and smile to enquiries about whether he is a good sleeper. For a baby, he probably is.

## Getting your baby to sleep

Sleeping and eating are two things that you cannot force your baby to do. It may take time, patience and being able to go with the flow before you can reach a happy compromise between your baby's sleeping needs and your own.

Very commonly, babies feed to sleep. Although this seems to be frowned upon by some, there is physiological evidence that this is normal and to be expected. A

*Photograph by Prue Carr*

hormone, called cholecystokinin (CCK) is released in both mother and baby at the end of a feed. This makes both feel sleepy. In the baby, this hormone peaks at the end of a feed, drops and then peaks again 30 to 60+ minutes later. This later peak is thought to be caused by the breastmilk, especially the fat, in the baby's stomach. So the baby sucks, dozes off and may wake again shortly, perhaps for a short top-up feed, before going into a deeper sleep.

Other ways of helping your baby sleep are rocking, or carrying in a sling. The motion, warmth and comfort of your body often help your baby drop off to sleep. A walk in the stroller or pram or a drive in the car may also help, although many babies usually wake once the car or pram stops.

Background noise is also helpful. Hum or sing a favourite song over and over, or use a radio, tape or loud ticking clock.

Many babies like to be tightly swaddled when put down to sleep alone, especially when on their backs, as is recommended. Babies have a natural startle response when lowered backwards or even just lying still on their backs, where their arms fling outwards and they seem frightened of falling. Swaddling suppresses this startle response and makes them feel more secure. In warm weather, use a light, open-weave fabric to avoid your baby over-heating.

If you feel you need to try to adjust your baby's balance of day and night sleeping, you could try shortening her daytime sleep, or try keeping her up later, so that she is more tired, and will perhaps sleep longer. Unfortunately, many parents report that this results in over-tiredness, leading to an even more disturbed night and an irritable baby the next day. They find that the baby sleeps better at night if she has had a good sleep during the day.

A set night-time routine of bath, story, breastfeed, a favourite toy and a song, a tuck-in and kiss can help settle an older baby. Usually, this is not effective until the baby is 12 months old.

It's a comfort for the parents of wakeful babies that they usually reach their developmental milestones earlier because they receive more stimulation, and are generally good company at a relatively young age. Babies whose parents respond to their crying promptly have been shown to settle better in the long

*Photograph by Amanda Radovic*

term because they are secure in the expectation that their needs are understood and met.

### try to remain calm

As far as possible, try to remain calm. Share the burden of getting up to a wakeful child; try to organise time for yourself so you can catch up on sleep, perhaps taking it in turns with your partner to go to bed early; eat well; and seek support from people you know will be sympathetic. Accept any help you can get with other chores. Reduce other stresses in your life as much as you can.

It is normal for your feelings of love and devotion to turn to despair and even anger if her crying is prolonged and, despite all your efforts, you are unable to comfort your baby. If you feel like this and fear that you may harm your baby, leave her safely in her cot for a few minutes and leave the room while you regain your equilibrium. A few minutes crying alone is less harmful to her than knowing that you may not be able to control your emotions at not being able to resolve the situation. Be reassured that sleep patterns change and this is usually only a temporary stage.

## Awake again?

There are many reasons why babies continue to wake. If this is the case with yours, it's worth looking at some of them. As he grows, his reasons for waking may change, and your attitude to his waking will also change.

- ○ Is it your first week at home? After an initial sleepy period, newborn babies can be unsettled a few days after birth, and after they arrive home. One of the reasons for this initial sleepiness is that colostrum contains casomorphins that help babies sleep to conserve energy. This effect wears off once he graduates to mature breastmilk. Time, a relaxed attitude and patience help your baby adjust.
- ○ Hungry? If your new baby wakes one to two hours after his last feed, he is probably hungry. Feeding is usually the quickest and most effective remedy.
- ○ Uncomfortable? Perhaps he is too hot, too cold, needs a nappy change or would prefer to be more or perhaps less snugly wrapped. It may take some time to find out your new baby's preferences. Perhaps he has been woken by a sudden sound and is frightened. Babies who sleep through daytime noise may become unsettled when the house is quiet. Try a soft tape or the radio on low.
- ○ Lonely? Babies are reassured by physical contact and may prefer to see you or be near you. Some cope better with solitude than others. Trying to teach him a lesson by resisting comforting him will only make a sensitive baby more insecure.

*Photograph by Susan D'Arcy*

- ○ Unwell? A sudden change to your baby's feeding and sleeping habits may indicate that he is ill. Check with your doctor. If medication is prescribed, ask about side effects as some medicines affect sleep.

○ Something you ate? Some breastfed babies are affected when their mothers eat or drink certain foods, or are taking medication. Discuss the problem with your doctor, child health nurse or an Australian Breastfeeding Association counsellor to help find the cause.

○ Teething? If your baby seems upset, is dribbling, drooling, has slight cold symptoms, seems to want to chew often and has swollen gums, he may well be teething. Teething symptoms sometimes appear for weeks before teeth erupt. He may be soothed by something cold rubbed on his gums, something to chew on, or if he is very distressed or ill, by medication. Consult your doctor before giving baby any teething medicine.

## Controlled crying/comforting

Sometimes well-meaning friends and relatives or some health professionals will advise you to let your baby 'cry it out' in the expectation that she will learn to go back to sleep by herself. Remember, though, that crying is your baby's means of communicating distress. She is not crying to wreck your evening, but because she needs something. Meeting her needs will not 'spoil' her. On the contrary, she will learn more quickly how to tell you what she wants and that the world is a secure and loving place. Without you to come to her aid when she cries, she is helpless.

Before you decide to let her cry it out, consider these questions. Is there an obvious reason for her crying? How do you feel about listening to it? How important is it to you to comfort your baby when she is scared or lonely? Will ignoring her cries solve or worsen the problem?

Some older children may respond to a program of 'controlled crying', although many children just become even more distressed. Professional assessment and support to sensitively implement this strategy are important, and remember that it is not usually considered appropriate until a child has some understanding of what her parents are saying — developmentally this happens around three years of age.

Given the recent proliferation of sleep training programs, it is worth noting the opinion of the Australian Association of Infant Mental Health as stated in its 2002 position paper on controlled crying. *The Association is concerned that the widely practised technique of controlled crying is not consistent with what infants need for their optimal emotional and psychological health, and may have unintended negative consequences.'* You can read the background to these concerns on this association's website (http://www.aaimhi.org/policies.html) before you make your own decisions on this issue.

## The family bed

The idea that babies must not intrude on the marital bed comes from a combination of Freud's ideas that this is unhealthy for the psychological development of the child, and the sexual relationship between husband and wife. However, Freud may have been the father of modern psychology, but he was never a mother. There are others who consider it is equally unhealthy for a tiny baby, newly emerged from the warmth and security of her mother's womb, to sleep alone. Many babies and parents sleep better when they sleep close to each other.

*Photograph by Dianne Griffiths*

The human animal (and then only in the Western world) is one of the few whose young sleep alone, and while this is in part because modern housing and heating mean that the infant does not need the warmth of her mother's body to survive the cold nights, there is no doubt that many mothers and babies enjoy the special closeness and security this brings. For centuries, mothers have slept with their babies, either in the same bed or in a cot next to the parents' bed, and still do in many parts of the world (including Australia).

Quite often there is a fear that once your baby begins to sleep with you, she will be there for years. There is little evidence to support this. If you can be relaxed about her presence, she will eventually decide of her own accord that her own bed is best.

To ensure that you do so safely, there are some points to consider if you choose to share a bed with your baby. Research shows that there may be a risk if you, or another person in the bed:
○ is a smoker (particularly if the baby is younger than four months).
○ is affected by drugs, alcohol or illness. This includes if the baby is ill.
○ is extremely obese or is so fatigued that they are unlikely to be aware of rolling onto the baby.
Some practical considerations:
○ The mattress should be firm and in good condition. Some types of waterbed are too soft.
○ Sleeping with your baby on a sofa, chair or saggy bed is not recommended as she could become wedged.

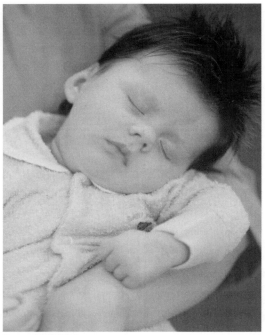

*Photograph by Vicki Bell*

❍ Make sure your baby doesn't get too hot. When dressing her for bed, take into account the warmth of the bedclothes and the radiated warmth from other bodies in the bed. Dress her in a similar thickness of clothing to you. Take care not to overheat the room.

❍ Remove soft bedding and pillows from where your baby will sleep. Some authorities suggest that sheets and blankets are safer than doonas or quilts.

❍ Don't wrap your baby tightly. She should be able to move freely.

❍ Ensure your baby can't fall out of the bed and can't get wedged anywhere.

❍ When breastfeeding, your baby may be on her side. When sleeping, it is suggested that you roll her onto her back.

❍ Make sure everyone in the house knows that your baby might be in your bed.

❍ It is not a good idea to leave your baby unattended in or on an adult bed.

❍ If another child sleeps in the same bed, it is best to have an adult between the child and the baby, to avoid the child rolling onto the baby.

❍ Pets should not share the bed with your baby.

Perhaps you have tried all these suggestions (and more) and they haven't worked. This may indicate that, like thousands of other parents awake at the same time, you cannot change your baby's in-built sleeping pattern. Take heart that it will change, given time, and is part of your baby's individuality.

*The most useful suggestion I ever heard was to just remind yourself that it won't last forever — it's only for a little while.*

# CHAPTER TWELVE

# A question of supply

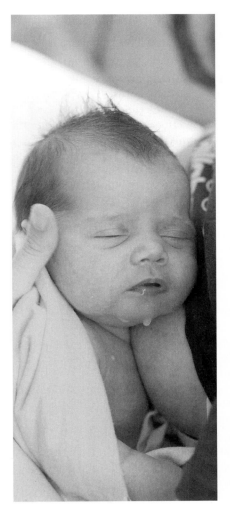

- *How to know if your supply really is low*
- *Some of the reasons for low supply*
- *How to make more milk*
- *Too much milk*
- *The pattern of breastfed babies' weight gains*

*An inadequate milk supply is rarely a problem if you understand the principle of supply and demand that governs the production of breastmilk.*

*Photograph by Davina Hurst*

'Not enough milk' is the most common reason cited for giving up breastfeeding. However, an inadequate milk supply is rarely a problem if you understand the principle of supply and demand that governs the production of breastmilk.

Photograph by Susan D'Arcy

## Is your supply actually low?

In some cases the real problem is a mother or her advisers not being properly informed about how to judge if a baby is getting enough. The checklist in Chapter Five is a good guide. Many mothers have a profound lack of confidence in their ability to provide enough breastmilk, so are over-anxious when their babies seem unsettled. Often, perfectly normal infant cues are misread as supply problems.

There are times when you can mistakenly believe that your milk supply has decreased:

○ When the early engorged feeling passes and your milk settles down to match your baby's needs.
○ When your baby needs more feeds than you were giving in hospital.
○ When your baby grows stronger and becomes expert at emptying the breast efficiently — often in just a few minutes.
○ In later months when you find your breasts are smaller.
○ When your baby is older and you may not feel your milk 'letting down' any more.
○ When the weather is hot and your baby is feeding more often to quench his thirst.
○ When your baby is unsettled even after being allowed to breastfeed for as long as he wants. Simple discomfort or even illness (an ear infection, thrush, teething) could be the cause.
○ When your baby has lots of wet and dirty nappies — more than ten wet and many dirty each day — and is continually unsettled and perhaps even colicky. While this situation is nearly always interpreted as not enough milk, it's usually a case of too much milk.
○ When a baby who has gained large amounts of weight in the early weeks (common in breastfed babies) suddenly changes to a slower gaining pattern, or a large baby's weight gain slows temporarily. It is common to see a plateau in weight gain around four months. The

charts in clinics are derived from a mixture of bottle-fed and breastfed babies and do not truly represent a breastfed baby's pattern of weight gain.

## Test weighing

Although it is still sometimes suggested to mothers who are concerned about their milk supply, test weighing is not recommended as it can be very misleading and undermining. Unless the weighing is done over a full 24-hour period or even longer, on reliable equipment, the results can be extremely variable and inaccurate. Breastfed babies take very different quantities of milk at each feeding. The volume of milk at one feed is not an adequate measure of how well your baby is being nourished.

If you have taken all these possibilities into account and you are still concerned, it's worth talking things over with a breastfeeding counsellor to see, firstly if you really have a problem, and secondly if it's a breastfeeding management problem. You might also consider seeing a lactation consultant who can check whether there are any anatomical problems affecting your baby's sucking. In the rare cases when none of these suggestions resolves the situation, talk to your medical advisers. There are some rare physical conditions that can prevent a baby from making the best use of breastmilk, or which can prevent your baby from sucking efficiently, or more usually it may be a problem unrelated to milk supply.

*Photograph by Vicki Bell*

# Reasons for low supply

Getting the supply-and-demand balance right is a matter of give and take. You and your baby need to work together to get the giving and the taking in correct balance. If you are concerned that you haven't got the balance right, there may be a number of factors involved.

## Feeding factors

❍ Inadequate stimulation of the breasts due to too-few feeds, too-short feeds or incorrect positioning. Your breasts need the stimulation of milk removal to make more milk. The more she removes from the breast, the

*Photograph by Susan D'Arcy*

more milk you will make. A baby who is fed on a schedule may not be stimulating the breast to make enough milk.

○ Changing sides before your baby has finished the first breast — that is setting an artificial time limit, then removing your baby from the breast, rather than watching for her signs.

○ Incorrect attachment or poor sucking technique of the baby at the breast. A baby who has not learnt to milk the breast correctly may not adequately stimulate the milk supply or may not get most of the milk available in the breast. This will result in inadequate fluid intake, few wet nappies, slow weight gains, a falling supply and possibly sore nipples. This is more common with some newborns; weak, sick or sleepy babies when they are not put to the breast early and often; or when the baby does not have to work for the milk because of a strong let-down reflex or oversupply. It may also happen if your baby has been confused about how to suck at the breast because she has been given bottles or dummies in the early days. If you think this is your baby's problem, talk to your Australian Breastfeeding Association counsellor, lactation consultant or child health nurse. They can help you learn how to encourage correct sucking techniques.

○ Regular use of complementary feeds will reduce your baby's demand for the breast, and will reduce your supply of milk. If you have been regularly using infant formula when leaving your baby, or to 'top up' after breastfeeds, your supply is likely to have decreased.

○ Your baby's demand for breastmilk will diminish if solids or fruit juices are introduced too soon, and your supply will drop. Breastmilk alone is the only food that your baby needs for at least the first six months. It is also the most nutritious. All other foods are inferior and less suited to your baby's digestive system.

○ In certain circumstances, stress has been shown to affect the let-down reflex and so may ultimately affect milk supply. This is thought to be because adrenaline (the stress hormone) restricts the size of blood vessels carrying oxytocin to the breast.

○ Mothers who return to paid work sometimes notice a drop in their milk supply if they use infant formula to complement or replace expressed breastmilk (EBM). More frequent feeds in the evenings and/or at weekends can overcome this.

## Mother-centred factors

○ When the balance of hormones in your body is undergoing change during ovulation or your period, your baby may not feed as well. Don't worry. He will usually make up for it when your hormones settle down again.

○ The use of a hormonal form of contraception, containing oestrogen, may cause your milk supply to drop. Breastfeeding mothers are usually only prescribed the progesterone-based contraceptives. However some mothers have reported that even these have caused their babies to be fussy. Frequent feeding is usually enough to offset the initial reaction in your baby. If not, you may need to discuss alternative methods of contraception.

○ If you become pregnant, your supply may decrease and your baby may become temporarily fussy at the breast. Some mothers prefer to wean at this time. However, with adequate diet and plenty of rest you can continue feeding if you choose to do so. The Australian Breastfeeding Association has a helpful booklet on breastfeeding through pregnancy (and beyond!).

○ Some drugs, both prescribed and over-the-counter, can affect breastfeeding, either by passing through the milk to your baby, or by affecting the process of lactation itself. Make sure you tell your doctor or pharmacist that you are breastfeeding and discuss the effects of any medication you are prescribed.

*Photograph by Lesley O'Donnell*

○ Research has shown that excessive amounts of alcohol, nicotine and caffeine (in tea, coffee, cola drinks, chocolate etc) may affect the let-down reflex and the production of milk or make your baby irritable or restless. Try to limit your consumption of these drugs while you are breastfeeding.

○ If you have been ill, or have undergone surgery, your milk supply may be lower. A bout of mastitis can also cause a sudden decrease in supply in the affected breast. Try to get plenty of rest and feed your baby frequently, both during your illness and after, and your milk supply will increase again.

○ It is highly unlikely that there is any physiological reason for a mother not to be able to produce enough milk for her baby. However, there are rare occasions when insufficient glandular tissue (which has nothing to do with the size of the breast), hormonal disturbances, or some types of previous breast surgery, and even retained placenta following the birth, may result in failure to produce enough breastmilk.

# How to make more milk

Remember: supply equals demand. If you want to make more milk, you need to create an environment in which your baby is able to feed often and well.

## Increasing your supply

○ Make sure your baby is correctly positioned and is attached well, and is feeding frequently. To maintain their supply, most mothers need to feed at least 8 and as often as 12 times in 24 hours. Not every feed will be of the same length — some may just be a quick snack and some will be long and leisurely and take a half hour or so. If you are at the low end of the number of feeds, offer the breast more often than usual for several days. Expressing, either by hand or pump after feeds, will maximise breast stimulation and emptying.

○ Try stroking the breast towards the nipple on all sides as your baby feeds, taking care not to dislodge the nipple from his mouth.

○ If your baby is sleepy and dozes off at the breast after only a few minutes, it may help to change sides several times during a feed, whenever his sucking slows and he starts to doze off. This can encourage babies to suck more strongly and so stimulates more let-downs. Wake and burp your baby as you switch sides to get the maximum amount of milk into him in the minimum amount of time, before he gets too sleepy to feed any more.

○ Offer little snack feeds when your baby is awake.

○ Offer the breast as a comforter for a few days instead of a dummy or thumb.

○ Go with the flow. If your baby is hungrier and wants to feed more often, do so. This is nature's way of increasing your supply to make sure the amount of milk you are making continues to match his needs.

○ Seek plenty of moral and practical support from your partner and others who can give it.

○ Rest whenever you are able and try to eat well. Do your best not to become stressed. Your health and wellbeing are important. Be kind to yourself. A day in bed or with the telephone off the hook can make a big difference.

○ Avoid giving water, juice or any other foods, unless there is a medical reason. These will lessen your baby's interest in breastfeeding and your supply will dwindle. On the other hand, he needs energy to feed well, so he may do better if he has a calorie boost. In most situations where a mother has had to give complementary feeds due to a low supply, with support and information from an Australian Breastfeeding Association counsellor, she is able to boost her supply and return to full breastfeeding. Some mothers who have actually weaned their babies have also been able to return to full breastfeeding.

*Photograph by Lesley McBurney*

*Nursing supplementer tubing on the breast*

○ Some women find a nursing supplementer, which allows the baby to stimulate the breast and obtain either infant formula or expressed breastmilk from a tube at the same time, helps build up a low supply. With the supplementer, a special container is worn around your neck. Fine tubing carries expressed breastmilk or formula from the container to the nipple. When your baby suckles the breast, milk is drawn through the tube into his mouth along with milk directly from the breast. Thoroughly cleaning the supplementer is time-consuming and some women find it awkward to use, but it can be invaluable in encouraging a baby to suckle while his mother tries to build her supply.

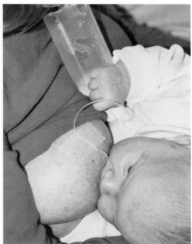

*Photograph by Yvette O'Dowd*

*Baby feeding with a nursing supplementer*

## Too much

While many mothers worry about whether they have enough milk for their babies, there are some mothers who worry about having enough baby for their milk. It usually takes at least six weeks for your breasts to adjust to the job of producing the right amount of milk for your baby at each feed, but occasionally a mother can have continuing problems with too much milk.

### Managing an oversupply

In most cases, the initial engorgement and oversupply of breastmilk settles over the first six weeks. If you continue to have too much milk as the weeks progress, there are several things you can do to reduce your supply.

It may help to feed from one breast at each feed, alternating breasts each time. Allow your baby to feed for as long as she needs on that breast. It may take her up to 30 minutes to get as much fat-rich hindmilk as she wants following the initial fast flow. Once your supply adjusts, you can go back to offering both breasts at each feed. Of course, your other breast can feel full and hard, particularly at the early morning feed, so you may need to gently express just enough to make yourself comfortable.

In some cases of extreme oversupply, it can sometimes help to feed from the one breast for two or more feeds in a row. This is just for a few days until your supply starts to settle down. And you always need to make sure that the unused breast isn't too full and that there are no signs of blocked ducts.

You may need to try scheduling feeds (say two-and-a-half- to three-hourly) to reduce the stimulation your breasts receive. The Australian Breastfeeding Association does not ordinarily recommend schedule-feeding and some babies can never be coaxed to accept it. If your baby does not accept this, try other methods of reducing your supply.

Also helpful may be:

○ expressing only when necessary for your comfort or to help your baby attach properly if your breast is too full or hard.

○ limiting the amount of non-nutritive sucking by using other soothing techniques such as rocking and even a dummy on occasions.

○ avoiding giving your baby extra fluids or solids as this will complicate your supply problems.

○ checking your breasts each day for signs of tightness or lumpiness, and massage or express lumps until they soften.

○ using cold packs to make your breasts feel more comfortable.

*Photograph by Susan D'Arcy*

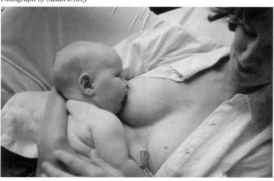

## A forceful let-down and fast flow

Sometimes, side effects of too much milk are a very forceful let-down reflex and fast flow of milk, so that your milk sprays out from both breasts, making your baby gag, splutter and sometimes pull away as your milk lets down. She may cry and fight the breast and may seem colicky and unsettled, especially in the early evening. She may have high weight gain. She will often have a bowel motion after each feed, and this may be green and frothy. She may bring up small amounts of milk after or between feeds, usually with a burp.

It should be noted, however, this is not *always* associated with an oversupply. Some mothers with normal supply have a very forceful let-down and fast flow. Their babies may gulp and gag at the beginning of a feed, but will settle as the feed progresses, and their weight gains will be adequate.

If forceful let-down and fast flow are a problem, there are a number of suggestions that you can try:

○ Trigger your let-down reflex by hand before you put your baby to the breast, catching the most forceful flow of milk in a nappy or cloth. This will help save your baby from being swamped with milk and encourage her to feed and empty the breast.

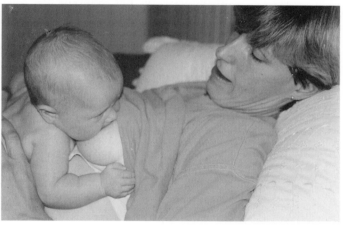

Photograph by Lesley McBurney

*Posture feeding*

○ Try feeding your baby while lying on your back with your baby on your tummy so that she is effectively sucking uphill, finishing the feed with you sitting up so the breasts are drained properly. This 'posture feeding' might help your baby cope with the fast flow of milk. Make sure your baby is attaching well, as this can be tricky in unusual positions. Some mothers find that just feeding lying down (both mother and baby on their sides) helps slow the flow a little, enough for baby to cope better.

○ Burp your baby after three to four minutes (after the fastest flow has subsided) and then put her back to finish her feed from that side. This can help to prevent wind problems.

○ Pay more attention to burping your baby after she finishes each side. Putting gentle pressure on her tummy can help expel air bubbles. If you think she is uncomfortable, rubbing her tummy or lower back with massage oil can help, as can rocking her or giving her a warm bath.

○ Persevere — these suggestions or a combination of them may need to be tried for a few days before you notice any real change.

# Weight gains

Most babies lose weight after birth and regain it within anything from a few days to two to three weeks. If your baby is slow to regain his birth weight, this is not an indication that your milk is inadequate. All babies are individuals and their growth rates are as variable as their personalities.

Although the focus on weight gains is not as obsessive now as it was in the past, regular weighing and measuring is still the most accepted and common way of monitoring your baby's growth in the first few years. Past and present ideas about weight gains often combine to paint a confusing picture for parents. On the one hand, you may be praised when your baby gains well, but on the other, if he is chubby, you may be warned that he is getting too much and that you should watch his diet! There is increasing concern about *over*weight problems in children and adults.

A baby who is being fed breastmilk alone for the first six months may sometimes appear chubby, but will not be obese, as there are no 'empty calories' in breastmilk. Breastfeeding allows babies to gain weight gradually as nature intended. Indeed breastfeeding has been shown to be an important preventative factor against many of the lifelong problems associated with weight management such as diabetes and heart disease.

### breastfed and bottle-fed babies' weight gain shouldn't be compared

A breastfed baby's pattern of weight gain may be very different from that of a bottle-fed baby and should not be compared. Generally speaking, breastfed babies gain weight the same as or faster than formula-fed babies in their first three to four months, and then the weight may plateau and the gains become steadier.

For an accurate picture of how your baby is growing, it is best to look at gains over the period of a month, rather than a week. Weekly gains

*Photograph by Joy Anderson*

may vary from 50 grams to 250 grams or more, depending on his rate of growth, hunger, or any illness, such as a cold. Some babies may gain as much as 400 grams a week, but on average, a gain of 500 grams a month is considered a good indicator of healthy growth. However, keeping your eye on charts and figures, rather than your baby, can sometimes be misleading.

If your baby is fully breastfed, is obviously growing well in length and head circumference, is alert and has good skin tone, then do not be too concerned if he is not gaining weight according to averages.

Inheritance plays a big part in determining your baby's size and growth rate. Your baby's birth and birth weight may also be factors in assessing weight gain. Babies grow towards their genetic growth curve over the first year.

A baby who was sick or premature may gain more slowly. On the other hand, a large baby may only make small but steady weight gains after birth, and a premature baby may make up for a slow start with larger weight gains.

*Photograph by Brooke Randell*

To make matters even more confusing, your baby's physical development now is not necessarily a good indicator of how he may look as an adult. All well-nourished babies have fat deposits on their cheeks (facial and otherwise), arms and legs and abdomens. This fat deposited during the relatively inactive time of babyhood is laid down in preparation for the very busy toddlerhood, when your baby will probably be interested in tasting everything, including sand and teabags, but will actually eat little. Before long, you will find that those charming little pork-sausage arms and legs have grown into long thin frankfurters as your child progresses from baby to toddler to young child.

Breastfeeding mothers seldom get caught in the trap of trying to force their baby to finish a bottle or worrying about how much he has had. And by waiting until he is six months old to introduce solids, your breastfed baby will be a more active participant in the feeding process, and you will get a better indication of when he is hungry and what he enjoys.

CHAPTER THIRTEEN

# Common breast conditions

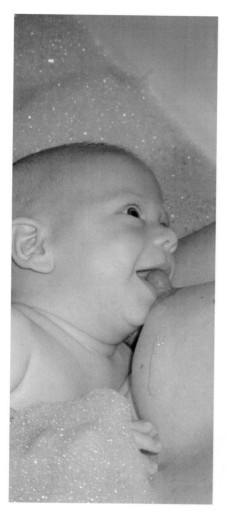

- *How to manage (or avoid) sore nipples*
- *Causes of nipple soreness beyond the first weeks*
- *Cracked nipples*
- *Thrush infection of the nipples*
- *Blocked ducts, mastitis and breast abscess*

*It may help you to know that there are many mothers who breastfed successfully for months or even years who began with similar problems.*

*Photograph by Stephen Smith*

The best way to ensure worry-free breastfeeding is to get accurate information and the support you need to prevent problems or to help resolve them quickly. Sometimes though, even with the best care, problems persist. They can be distressing and discouraging. If your breasts or nipples are tender or painful as you read this; if feeding your baby has become an endurance test rather than an enjoyable experience, you may be wondering whether it is all worth it. Often weaning is seen as a quick fix and is presented to mothers as the only sensible option.

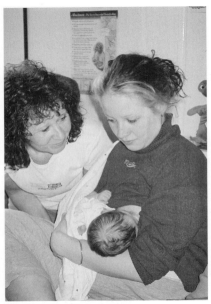

*Photograph by Martine Kimpton*

However, most women report feelings of intense sadness at having weaned before experiencing a happy breastfeeding relationship. In most cases weaning is not the best solution.

Sometimes the solution to your problem can be as simple as feeding your baby more often. At other times you may need to try several different suggestions before your problem is resolved. It may help you to know that there are many mothers who breastfed successfully for months or even years who began with similar problems to your own and who felt equally discouraged. You will find that in your local Australian Breastfeeding Association group, or among relatives and friends, other mothers are keen to tell you how they overcame any problems they may have had. Their stories are meant to encourage and inspire you, not intimidate you. Becoming a mother for the first or even the fifth time can be an exciting, but sometimes stressful experience. Breastfeeding should be one of the joys, not one of the stresses.

## Sore nipples

Ultimately, breastfeeding should not hurt. It takes a little while to get used to the strong sucking of a healthy baby, so when you begin breastfeeding, your nipples will be sensitive and you can expect some initial nipple tenderness.

Sometimes mothers are still advised to limit the feed times to start with, to minimise this early discomfort. However, research now shows that restricting your baby's time at the breast can also lead to a build-up of milk and increased engorgement, which may result in even more soreness. Taking care in getting your baby on and off your breast, some simple first-aid treatment, and a little time and patience are usually all that is needed to solve the problem. You will find that sore nipples improve quickly once you learn how to attach your baby correctly to the breast.

## Reducing (and avoiding) nipple soreness

### before feeds

One way of reducing soreness is to feed your baby more often, as she will be calmer when she comes to the breast, be easier to attach and will suck more gently. If you find that your nipples hurt most at the beginning of a feed, before your milk lets down, you may find it helpful to gently massage your breast and express some milk beforehand. This will get the milk flowing and soften the areola so that your nipple is easier for your baby to grasp. The milk will also lubricate your nipple allowing it to slide more easily into your baby's mouth.

If you find yourself dreading each feed, try to consciously relax to help you cope with the pain. Pain relieving medication may help if you think you need it. Make sure you are sitting or lying comfortably and bring your baby to your breast. Don't move forward to put your nipple into her mouth. Once she is attached properly and the milk starts flowing, the pain usually disappears. If it doesn't, it may be necessary to check your baby's attachment again. If you need to re-attach your baby, first break the suction by putting a (clean) finger into the corner of her mouth rather than just wrenching your nipple from it.

*Photograph by Susan D'Arcy*

### while feeding

Feed from the less-sore side first. This will take the edge off your baby's hunger and make sure that your milk is flowing freely when she attaches to the sore nipple.

When you take your baby from your breast, check your nipple. You may notice a line of swelling and redness across the nipple, a white area or even a small stripe of blood under the skin. Or the nipple may

Photograph by Prue Carr

Photograph by Yvette O'Dowd

*Underarm or twin position (above)*

*Lying down position (at left)*

appear squashed or ridged as it comes out of her mouth. These are signs that your nipple is stressed by your baby's sucking and her attachment could be improved.

Check that your baby is taking your breast correctly. Changing her position for part of the feed may help. Try feeding lying down on your side, or use the twin position, holding your baby under your arm against your body on the side from which she is feeding, her head facing your nipple and her feet behind you. You still need to check that your nipple and a good portion of the underside of your areola are well in her mouth, her chin is pressed into your breast and her lips are turned out.

While your baby is small, it may help to support her with extra pillows. This helps keep the nipple in her mouth and prevents her pulling back and stretching it. However, take care not to raise your baby's body too high. Her mouth should be level with the natural height of your nipple, so that you are not lifting your breast to her level.

Most babies need to comfort suck and it also helps to remove more of the very nourishing hindmilk from the breast. However, if your nipples are sore, you may like to shorten her comfort sucking time by letting her satisfy this need by sucking on your finger. You could also try rocking, cuddling and patting her. If this does not work, another short feed half an hour or so later will probably settle her.

*after feeds*

Express a few drops at the end of the feed and smear the milk over your nipple, and let it dry by leaving your bra open for a few minutes. This hindmilk is high in fat and has anti-infective and healing properties. There is no need to wash your nipples before and after each feed as this can dry the skin. It's best to leave the natural oils to do their job. Specially-designed breast shells or nipple protectors can be worn inside your bra to allow air to circulate around your nipples while protecting them from clothing that may rub.

Most breastfeeding authorities recommend that nipple creams are unnecessary unless they are medically prescribed for specific conditions. Creams and other preparations can sometimes worsen rather than cure problems. They can also harbour germs and other organisms such as thrush.

You should avoid using anything on your nipples that might damage delicate nipple skin, such as soaps, shampoos or harsh towels. Make sure your bras are well-fitting and that, if you use nursing pads, they don't hold moisture against the skin. Be careful in both your choice and use of breast pumps. If you must use a nipple shield in the short-term, make sure you do so with the assistance of a lactation specialist.

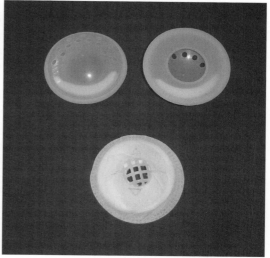

*Photograph by Joy Anderson*

*Rigid breast shells, showing outer and inner parts, and absorbent material inside (top of photo) and nipple protector fitted into a cut breast pad (bottom of photo)*

## Later nipple soreness

Although nipple soreness is most common early in a lactation, sore nipples can occur at any time during breastfeeding, for a host of reasons. Heavy babies held loosely on the lap can drag on the nipples. Acrobatic and inquisitive older babies may turn and twist the breast without letting go, stretching the nipple. Babies who sleep at the breast and hold onto the nipple sometimes bite to catch it if they feel it sliding out.

Teething babies can sometimes bite to relieve gum tenderness. Give your baby something hard and cold to chew on before a feed. Some mothers feel that changes to their babies' saliva during teething can irritate their nipples. Try rinsing the nipple area with a little bicarbonate of soda dissolved in water (about one teaspoon to one cup).

Hormonal changes, caused by menstruation, ovulation or pregnancy can also cause nipple tenderness.

## Dermatitis or infection

The sudden onset of severe sore nipples when feeding an older baby, or indeed prolonged nipple soreness at any stage should be investigated to rule out a medical condition. If your nipples are red, itchy or sore to the touch, or if the skin on the nipple and areola looks scaly or flaky, it may be a sign that there is a medical problem such as dermatitis, or a thrush or bacterial infection. Dermatitis can occur as a result of an allergic reaction to a nipple cream or to soaps, shampoos or detergent residues in clothing. Stop using the suspect substances until you sort out the cause. Try washing your bras with pure soap and rinse well.

## White spot

Occasionally, a tiny white blister may appear on the nipple, about the size of a pin-head or sometimes a little larger. Often the area around the spot is inflamed, red and painful, usually throughout the feed. This is a fairly rare condition, commonly called white spot, which often resolves itself. It may be associated with a blocked duct and mastitis. Position your baby carefully to minimise pressure on the sore spot. Apply warmth to the area and hand express to clear the spot. Sometimes the covering skin can be removed, usually with a sterile needle. It's important that this is done carefully to minimise the risk of infection, so is best done by your medical adviser.

## Nipple vasospasm

Nipple vasospasm is described as a sharp pain, burning or stinging of the nipple and is accompanied by sudden whitening of the nipple followed by a colour change from red to blue. In many cases, mothers have a history of Raynaud's phenomenon, a condition where an individual has an extreme sensitivity to cold, particularly in the hands and feet. If it only occurs in response to feeding, nipple vasospasm is most likely a sign that the nipple is being stressed and damaged as a result of incorrect attachment. It can also occur when there is a thrush infection on the nipples. If these underlying causes are treated, the vasospasm should stop. If it is occurring between feeds, keeping your breasts warm and applying localised warmth may help alleviate symptoms.

# Cracked nipples

Sore nipples, if properly managed, usually improve quickly. However, if sore nipples are left untreated, they can develop fissures, commonly called cracks. Sometimes you can see the crack on the tip of the nipple or where the nipple joins the areola, but sometimes it is too fine to be seen easily. Feeding is usually very painful and may even cause bleeding. It is reassuring to know that although bleeding may look alarming, and blood may even show up in your baby's bowel motions or regurgitated milk, it isn't harmful and it is quite safe to keep breastfeeding. An excessive amount of blood in the feed may cause the baby to vomit, as it irritates the stomach, but this is not harmful to the baby.

In most cases, cracked nipples are the result of incorrect positioning and attachment and they heal quickly once this is corrected. There are other possible causes to look at if you believe you have your baby well attached.

Cracks can be caused, or made worse, by medical conditions such as thrush, bacterial infection or dermatitis, or by the incorrect use of breast pumps. The shape of your baby's mouth can sometimes be a factor, so ask your paediatrician or a lactation consultant to check this if you are concerned.

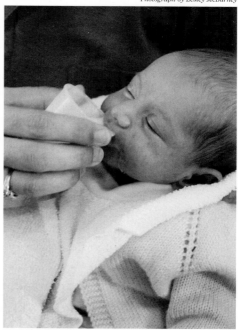

*Cup-feeding*
*Photograph by Lesley McBurney*

## First aid for cracked nipples

The first aid measures described in the section on sore nipples help cracked nipples as well. Many mothers are able to continue to feed through cracked nipples; however some find this too painful or that the crack worsens. As a last resort, your baby may have to be taken off the breast temporarily. Express your milk by hand or with a good-quality breast pump on a gentle setting, to rest the nipple until it begins to heal. You can feed your expressed milk to your baby by cup.

Make sure you drain the breast well. Because bacteria can enter through the crack, and an infection may follow, pay scrupulous attention to keeping anything that comes in contact with the nipple as clean as possible. Smear some hindmilk onto your nipple after expressing. This will act as both an anti-infective agent and a soothing

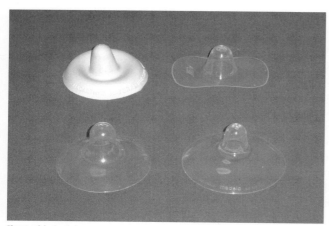

Photograph by Joy Anderson

*Some of the nipple shields available*

lubricant. As soon as the crack has improved, gradually reintroduce the breast, taking special care to get your baby's attachment as perfect as possible. Start each feed on the good side. Check your sore nipple after each feed. Continue to express from that breast and use the milk to top up your baby until you are back to full feeding.

If neither feeding directly at the breast nor expressing is working, you might need to try a soft nipple shield. There is a variety of these available, and you may find that some are likely to fit your unique size and shape better than others. Some mothers find that the friction of a shield on the nipple while the baby is feeding makes the pain worse or that use of the shield leads to supply problems. Use them with caution, with the ongoing advice of a lactation consultant or breastfeeding counsellor and 'wean' your baby off them as soon as you can.

## Thrush

If your nipples suddenly become sore after a period of comfortable feeding, and if breastfeeding your baby causes sharp, excruciating, radiating breast pain, you may have thrush. This is a yeast-like organism which occurs naturally in the digestive tract, but which can cause infection in the breast.

Thrush in the nipples can come as a surprise to some women who may be (unfortunately) familiar with vaginal thrush, but may not be aware that it can also be present on the nipples and in the breast.

Nipple thrush is most likely to occur if you have a cracked nipple that allows the infection to penetrate. The pain is often totally out of proportion to the damage that can be seen.

### Signs and symptoms

Signs of nipple thrush may include redness, shiny areas, flaking or white spots, or there may be no obvious outward signs at all. Symptoms include itching, knife-like pain, burning, deep pain or throbbing in the breast, sometimes extending to the arm or back. As well as being sore, your nipples will be very sensitive to the touch and you may not be able to bear having your clothes rub on them.

## Treating thrush

If your medical adviser diagnoses thrush you will be prescribed an antifungal treatment. Be sure to check how long you should continue with treatment. It is usually necessary to continue for some time after the symptoms have stopped. In some severe cases, tablets may be prescribed. Your doctor will also check your baby's mouth for white curd-like spots or coating which does not come off when scraped with a finger. His mouth will usually be treated at the same time, even if there is little evidence of thrush there.

Thrush can be transferred from your vagina to your baby's mouth if you have an infection during childbirth, and from his mouth to your nipple and vice versa. That is why it's important for all possible sources of infection to be treated at the same time. Your partner may also have to be treated if it is suspected he is also harbouring thrush. Even if you have not resumed intercourse, any sexual contact may cause the infection to pass from penis to hand to mouth and to nipple and back again.

Scrupulous attention to hygiene is vital in getting rid of thrush. Wash your hands before and after feeds, nappy changes, and wash towels, face washers and bras frequently. Boil any toy, teat or dummy that your baby sucks, and change teats and dummies regularly. Cold-water disinfectant solutions are less efficient at killing thrush than boiling.

Some women also find a low-yeast or low-carbohydrate diet helps, or eating natural, unsweetened yoghurt, which contains acidophilus, or taking other special acidophilus preparations. These help colonise your bowel with 'good' bacteria and assist your immune system to deal with thrush organisms in other parts of your body. However, consult your medical adviser or a dietitian before you make any major changes to your diet.

There is no reason to stop breastfeeding if you have thrush. Your own treatment will not affect baby's desire or ability to feed. If your baby is affected too, the thrush in his mouth may temporarily make him reluctant to feed, but once it's treated he will regain his appetite and enthusiasm.

Some research into ongoing, severe nipple soreness suggests that what was assumed to be thrush, but has proved to be 'resistant' to medical treatment may actually be bacterial infection, usually a staphylococcal infection. So if thrush treatment is not working after a few days to a week, consult your medical adviser again, in case there is a different infection present that needs to be treated.

# Blocked ducts

If you have a lumpy or engorged area on your breast, which feels sore or looks red, you probably have a blocked duct. Sometimes a duct (which carries milk from the glands in the breast) becomes compressed or narrowed and blocked. Milk ducts, on average, are only 2 mm in diameter, so it's easy to see how blockages can occur from time to time.

Milk then banks up behind the blockage, a lump forms and your breast begins to feel sore.

You should start treatment immediately, otherwise your breast may become inflamed and you may begin to feel feverish. See your medical adviser if this happens or you can't clear the blocked duct within 12 hours.

*Photograph by Yvette O'Dowd*

## Treating blocked ducts

❍ Start treatment immediately.
❍ Feed from the affected breast first, when your baby is sucking vigorously.
❍ Feed more frequently than usual, starting each feed from the affected breast and let your baby feed as long as possible on this side. However, it's important to ensure that the unaffected breast doesn't become overfull.
❍ Apply warmth before a feed. Heat is comforting and helps clear a blockage by encouraging the let-down reflex. You can have a warm shower or immerse your breasts in comfortably-warm water in the bath or a basin. If this sounds like too much trouble, you can use a well-covered hot-water bottle, or a warm towel or face washer wrung out in very warm water, or a commercial heat pack, taking great care not to burn your sensitive breast skin.
❍ To help shift the blockage, gently but firmly massage the lump towards the nipple during and after feeds, and also perhaps in the bath or shower.

○ Change feeding positions to help drain the breast. If you choose positions that allow the milk to flow 'downhill' to your baby, gravity helps the flow. So feeding while lying on your left side might help a blockage on the right side of either nipple. If the blockage is under the nipple, raise the breast with your opposite hand while you feed. Crazy as it sounds, you can even try feeding on all fours.

○ Hand express if necessary to ensure your breasts are well drained.

○ Loosen your bra, or better still, take it off during feeds.

○ Use cold packs after a feed to relieve pain and minimise inflammation.

○ Rest as much as possible.

○ See your medical adviser if you cannot clear the lump in 12 hours or if you begin to feel unwell.

*Photograph by Yvette O'Dowd*

If you have previously had breast surgery, you will need to be particularly careful to check for blockages while breastfeeding. The ease with which you will be able to breastfeed your baby will depend on the reason for the surgery (for example, if tissue was removed or implants inserted), the size and location of the incision and any scar tissue. Many women who have had surgery are able to feed successfully. Even if one breast cannot be used at all, a baby can usually be fed successfully from the other.

## Mastitis

Mastitis literally means an inflammation of the breast. While it is commonly believed that any mastitis is a breast infection, the redness, pain and heat in the breast isn't necessarily linked to a bacterial infection. Most cases of mastitis begin with a blockage of a milk duct in the breast. You may develop a high temperature, chills, aches and other flu-like symptoms. If there is no bacterial infection, and you only have the localised symptoms, you may be able to treat the problem by frequent feeding, rest and applying warmth to the tender area just before

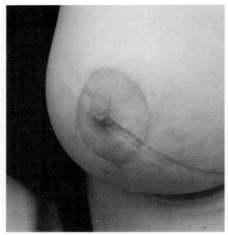

*Photograph by Michael McBurney*

feeding your baby, and cold packs afterwards and between feeds.

## What causes mastitis?

There is thought to be a number of factors that increase your chances of developing mastitis, including:

○ an unresolved blockage in a milk duct or nipple opening.

○ regularly missing feeds, infrequent feeds, scheduling feeds or restricting the duration of feeds.

○ poor attachment, so that some areas of your breast are not being drained well at each feed.

○ cracked or grazed nipples (usually resulting from poor attachment).

○ an oversupply of milk.

○ rapid weaning.

○ pressure on areas of the breast, most commonly from a poorly-fitting bra, restrictive clothing, using pressure on the breast during a feed or even car seatbelts, from sleeping on your tummy, and for some, simply wearing a bra to bed.

○ any injury to a breast or previous breast surgery.

○ if you are sick, very tired and stressed.

## Treating mastitis

***Don't stop breastfeeding!*** Effective removal of breastmilk is the most important step towards recovering from a bout of mastitis. It's a common myth that you shouldn't breastfeed during a bout of mastitis. This is definitely not true! There is no evidence that your milk poses a health risk to your baby. Your breastmilk has antibacterial properties to protect your baby.

Letting the milk bank up in the breast will make the condition much worse, so you should feed frequently, beginning each feed on the affected breast. If the pain in the sore breast is so severe that your let-down is affected, start with the other breast and swap as soon as your milk begins to flow. Varying the feeding position helps to drain all the areas of the breast. Gently massaging the breast towards the nipple during the feed, as well as finishing each feed by expressing some remaining milk, can also help breast drainage and speed up the recovery process. Applying warmth to the sore breast before you feed can be very comforting.

Take time to rest, allowing yourself time off from work (and that means housework too). If possible, rest in bed with your baby close to you so you don't have to get up and down. Have everything you might need at hand including a glass and a jug of water and a nutritious snack.

## Medication

If you have tried all these strategies over the past 24 hours and things are not improving, or if it's only been a few hours and you are feeling extremely unwell, you should quickly consult your medical adviser, who will probably prescribe antibiotics. Your doctor will be able to prescribe a medication that is compatible with breastfeeding and may also suggest a painkiller to help with the aches and pains. Even if the mastitis is non-infective, and it is impossible for your doctor to be able to tell whether it is or not, antibiotics will help as they have an anti-inflammatory action, which reduces symptoms. If an antibiotic is prescribed, finishing the course will help you avoid a recurrence of the problem.

### prevention is better than cure

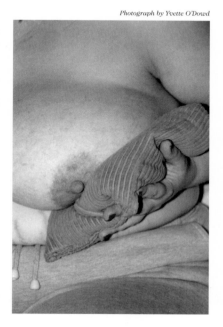

*Photograph by Yvette O'Dowd*

As with most breastfeeding problems, prevention is better than cure, so it will help if you keep a lookout for any telltale signs while following some simple tips.

○ Make sure your baby is well positioned at every feed to drain each breast effectively.
○ Don't restrict either the number or length of feeds.
○ Express after a feed if your baby hasn't fed well and your breasts still feel very full.
○ Check your breasts each day for signs of lumps, redness or nipple damage.
○ If they become tender, apply some warmth to the breast before feeds and gently massage away any lumpy areas while feeding. Apply some cold after the feed to reduce inflammation.
○ Get as much rest as you can, particularly in the first three months.
○ Don't smoke — it lowers your resistance to infection.

## Breast abscess

A breast abscess is a localised collection of pus that forms when a bacterial infection hasn't drained. It is usually a complication of infective mastitis that has been poorly treated, and particularly where a mother has weaned during a bout of breast inflammation. Symptoms of a breast abscess include nausea, extreme fatigue and aching muscles, in addition to swelling, pain and redness in the affected area. A breast abscess requires surgical drainage as well as antibiotic therapy and rest. It's important that you keep the breast well drained.

CHAPTER FOURTEEN

# Tummy troubles

*Photograph by Simone Hanckel*

*Find someone calming that you feel comfortable with and engage their help. A problem shared is a problem halved.*

- The difference between wind and colic
- Ideas for soothing and comforting your colicky baby
- Gastric reflux
- Lactose intolerance
- Allergies

Some babies have a greater sensitivity to gastrointestinal problems than others. Seeing your baby distressed and in pain is enormously stressful, as you struggle to work out exactly what's wrong and how you can help. The term 'colic' is used to describe a wide range of abdominal pains, but should not be confused with 'wind'. Although both include pain and crying, colic causes much more intense crying and in severe cases may require medical treatment. Sometimes gastro-oesophageal reflux is confused with colic, as they both cause great distress in babies.

Photograph by Sylvie Jackson

## Wind

Wind generally refers to the bubble of air brought up during or soon after a feed. Unless the flow of milk is too fast, a baby can safely swallow and breathe alternately about once a second. Some babies seem to accumulate more air during feeding than others.

Everyone swallows air when they eat, and this is not always a problem. In fact, in some cultures burping babies is seen as an eccentric and unnecessary practice. Babies often make strange faces and seem to be considerably uncomfortable. This is entirely normal and doesn't necessarily mean your baby is in pain or has colic. He is just getting used to these new sensations as his digestive system springs into action.

To help your baby bring up wind, you might just have to hold him upright and the excess bubble of wind will rise from the stomach. Or you can hold him comfortably against your shoulder so that the upper part of his tummy fits into it. Gently rub or pat his back. You may also lie your baby on his back, his body flat on your knees for about a minute, then raise him gently to sitting position, keeping his back straight. Another popular position for burping is to sit your baby on your lap, supporting his chin with your hand, and with your other hand on his back. Some babies will reward you with an adult-size burp, others will never seem to bring up much wind.

# Colic

If your baby has colic, he may begin at first to squirm and fuss, sucking at his hands and showing all the signs of hunger, yet when you put him to the breast, he will feed eagerly for a few minutes, then stop and cry or scream. He may settle for a short while, only to wake again crying.

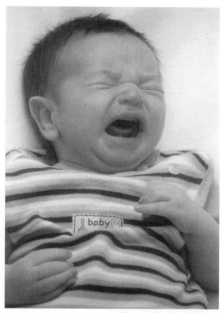

During colic attacks, his face will probably redden, his brow will furrow and his pupils may dilate as if he is frightened. He may draw his legs to his tummy, crying with sharp, shrill yells. Picking him up seems to offer little comfort. He stops crying only when the spasm ends. Each attack may last four or five minutes, and although a baby may drift off to sleep he is soon woken with another attack. This may be repeated many times, causing distress and exhaustion for the whole family. Sometimes the symptoms are accompanied by loud tummy gurgles, frequent burping or breaking of wind. This may give him some relief, as does passing a bowel motion or

*Photograph by Amanda Radovic*

sucking. The desire to suck sometimes leads mothers to misinterpret colic as hunger.

## What causes colic?

No-one really knows what causes colic. One theory supported by research suggests that the baby who is switched to the second breast too early may not take enough of the fat-rich milk because fat content increases as a feed progresses. This means he has taken in too little fat and more lactose than can be efficiently broken down. The excess lactose moves from the small bowel into the large bowel, and the bacteria in the large bowel ferment the lactose. This fermentation process produces gas that causes colic, wind and frequent loose and sometimes explosive bowel actions. If there is sufficient fat in the breastmilk, this slows down the gastric-emptying time and the overall speed that the food takes to travel through the digestive system. Therefore more time allows the lactose to be better digested. A baby who takes large, low-fat feeds may still act like he is hungry, frequently wanting to suck, and so further contributing to the problem of colic.

Other research shows that a small number of babies seem to react to

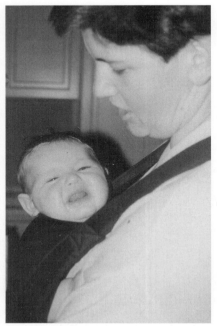

*Photograph by Lesley McBurney*

some foods in their mothers' diets, for instance some babies are particularly sensitive to caffeine, which is found in tea, coffee, chocolate and cola drinks. When these mothers cut out caffeine, their babies no longer cried as much. Any significant change in your diet (eg giving up dairy products) should only be done under the care of a dietitian or allergy specialist. It's a process that is only effective when done properly and you need to be sure you are still getting a balanced diet.

Yet another theory is that colic is a consequence of a baby receiving too much stimulation — a sensory overload. These babies need quiet surroundings and soothing, calm handling until their colic resolves.

## Soothing and comforting your colicky baby

First of all, be reassured that this difficult time won't last forever, and that most colicky babies seem to gain weight well. Rest assured too that your breastmilk is still the best food for your baby. Infant formula is not as easily digested as breastmilk and formula-fed babies suffer with colic too. As your baby grows, his digestive system will mature. In the meantime, there are a number of things you might try to provide some measure of comfort.

○ Try to make his feed times as gentle and relaxing as possible. Feed him before he actually reaches the point of crying to be fed.
○ Walk with him, as this rocks him naturally. Crying, colicky babies are seldom seen in countries where babies are carried around until they can walk. An Australian Breastfeeding Association baby sling will allow you to carry your baby upright and keep your hands free. Being taken for a ride and watching you go about your day will also distract him from his discomfort.
○ Wrapping him snugly in a warm, softly-textured material, such as cotton or light wool can help comfort him.
○ Colicky babies prefer being upright and/or to have pressure on their tummies.
○ Some colicky babies cry in their sleep without waking. Wait to see if he drifts back to sleep before you pick him up, but don't let him get distressed. It is probably best to have him sleep near you so you can watch and assess whether he needs to be left alone or be comforted.

○ A dummy can help an older baby who gets his main comfort from sucking, but whose constant suckling is causing an overabundance of milk. However this will not work if your baby is hungry, and while it is a good substitute for the breast in this circumstance, it is not a good substitute for you. He will still need the comfort of your arms, even if he has a dummy. Sucking is good for colicky babies as it helps expel the gas by moving it through the bowel.

○ If you have an overabundance of milk, as shown by more than ten wet nappies and many bowel motions a day, feed your baby on only one side per feed, or if he wants to suck frequently, offer the same side for two or more feeds in a row. Watch for blockages in the unused breast. You may only need to do this for a few days before returning to a more normal feeding pattern.

○ If your let-down reflex is very strong, your baby may be struggling to cope with the flow. It can help if you express some milk before a feed, waiting until the initial rush of milk has subsided before offering him the breast.

○ 'Posture feeding', or feeding so that your baby is sucking against gravity, is one way of slowing the flow. Some mothers say an early-morning posture feed helps ease colic. You can do this by attaching him as usual while sitting, then lying back with your baby on your tummy. (See page 119.) Remember to finish the feed sitting up, so that all the milk ducts are drained.

*Thank goodness for the invention of the Meh Tai sling. My baby's colic disappeared while he was in that sling.*

*An evening deep bath on the kitchen table with the heater on, dim lights and a short massage before the final feed of the night often helped relax my baby, and me.*

## Other tips for soothing your baby

○ Raise the bassinette at the head end. This helps the bubble of wind to rise.

○ Let your baby kick on the floor for a while, or you can exercise her legs for her with a gentle bicycle action.

○ Baby massage can be incredibly relaxing and comforting for all babies, but especially babies suffering from colic.

○ Check that the room is comfortably warm, but avoid overheating.

○ A warm bath, or shower with a parent, often helps babies relax.

○ A change of scenery, a stroll in the garden or around the block can relax you both.

○ Try gentle movement in a pram or stroller. Roll the pram back and

forth as you sit or stand. Providing a slight bump, such as a folded towel, to roll over sometimes helps, or use a doorway where there is a change in floor coverings — the join will provide a gentle bump.

○ Rhythmic, continuous 'white noise', such as the drone of the washing machine or a vacuum cleaner can help lull your baby to sleep. A radio, just off a station, is another way to create 'white noise' — that's if you can stand it!

○ Music with a soft melody or something with a definite beat, or singing to your baby can be distracting.

Be easy on yourself. This period will pass, but until it does, focus on your baby's needs and your own needs rather than those of the household. Enlist the help of others in meal preparation and shopping; fight fatigue by resting whenever you can; try to find some time to relax or do something you enjoy. If you're an Australian Breastfeeding Association subscriber, your local group will also provide you with support.

If colic continues, have your baby checked regularly by your medical adviser to ensure that she is growing well. Most colicky babies thrive and the colic passes. Meanwhile, focus on soothing your baby and getting as much support and encouragement for yourself as possible.

## Gastric reflux

Nearly all babies bring up a little milk now and again. This 'posetting' or regurgitating is often accompanied by a burp, and is a baby's way of coping with overflow. Apart from the fact that it usually occurs on somebody's shoulder just after they have changed into something clean or special, it poses no problem. Although it may look as if your baby has just thrown up her dinner, this is not vomiting.

However, there are some babies that seem to have a fountain inside. What goes down does not stay down for long and inevitably seems to come up. If your baby does this repeatedly, a paediatrician will need to diagnose whether your baby is simply regurgitating, has gastric reflux or some other gastrointestinal condition. If she needs to take a medication for reflux, a number of different medications can be prescribed that are safe for your breastfed baby.

Some babies are 'happy chuckers' while others will be quite distressed. Gastric reflux, also known as gastro-oesophageal reflux, is sometimes confused with colic, as some babies suffer heartburn when the stomach acids rise in the lower part of the oesophagus. Not all babies with gastric reflux vomit, some arch their backs in an attempt to escape from the pain of heartburn, but vomiting is the most common symptom.

Sometimes the milk oozes up, while at other times it seems to be projected with the force of a hose. A baby may even bring up milk long after the end of a feed, after being asleep for some time.

Photograph by Lesley McBurney

*Upright feeding positions can help babies with reflux*

Babies with gastric reflux may also be poor sleepers, waking easily and frequently, sometimes screaming after being laid down. Crying and irritability, especially during feeding or after a feed are other symptoms, as are feeding difficulties, either frequent feeding — or alternately — breast refusal, snuffles, a dry cough and hiccoughs that distress the baby.

Apart from the distress and mess this can cause, in occasional babies the amount of milk lost can cause weight loss and failure to thrive. Most gastric reflux is mild and disappears as a baby matures, settling down when she spends more time sitting or standing upright. By the age of 12–18 months, after they begin walking, most babies show no symptoms.

If your baby is diagnosed with gastric reflux, it is better for both of you if you continue to breastfeed. Babies fed on infant formula risk further complications if they inhale traces of the formula after vomiting. Reflux is often associated with allergies, which are more common in formula-fed babies.

*Find someone calming that you feel comfortable with and engage their help. A problem shared is a problem halved.*

### Some practical suggestions

The suggestions for babies with colic can work equally well for babies with gastric reflux. You could also try:

○ Settling your baby before feeding. Irritable babies are more likely to vomit.

○ Propping him on pillows to keep him relatively upright while you change his nappy. Avoid pressure on the stomach from tight nappies or pants. Short periods in a reclining baby chair may help but don't allow him to slump over, as this puts more pressure on his tummy.

○ The constant cleaning up and washing, accompanied by the distress of your baby, frequent night waking, worry about his weight gains and the need to carry him upright to help him keep his feeds down, will take its toll on both you and your partner. In some parts of Australia, there are special support groups for parents living with a baby with reflux.

## Lactose intolerance

The primary form of this is a very rare condition where the lactose in milk — the main carbohydrate component in all mammals' milk — cannot be digested by the baby. The main symptoms are watery,

*Photograph by Sylvie Jackson*

acidic diarrhoea, wind, a distended abdomen and failure to thrive. The symptoms in the vast majority of cases diagnosed as lactose intolerance are due to subtle damage to the digestive system lining, for example following a bout of gastroenteritis, especially a rotavirus infection, or an allergy or intolerance to a food protein in the mother's milk, originating from her diet.

The enzyme lactase, needed to digest lactose, is produced in the very tips of folds in the intestine, and anything that causes damage to the gut may wipe off these tips and reduce the enzyme production. Lactose intolerance should be medically diagnosed and the underlying cause investigated and treated. Recovery may take a little time, but you should be able to continue breastfeeding.

Many breastfed babies produce multiple, loose bowel motions and this should not be confused with lactose intolerance. A baby who is switched from one breast to the other without the chance to drain the first breast may sometimes show symptoms similar to lactose intolerance, but this is actually lactose overload rather than intolerance. Allowing the baby to drain the breast usually overcomes this. A mother with an oversupply of breastmilk may also see these symptoms in her baby.

## Allergies

If you or your partner suffer from any allergic conditions, you may be concerned that you will pass the condition on. A small number of babies are sensitive to particular foods, even through their mothers' milk. Sensitisation can occur both before birth as well as after, as allergens can cross the placenta. In the early months, your baby's digestive system is immature,

*Photograph by Lesley McBurney*

allowing foreign proteins to transfer into the body more easily than when she is older. This can increase the risk of sensitisation.

This is why giving babies infant formula complements soon after birth is thought to predispose those at risk to cows'-milk allergy, even if they are later fully breastfed.

Studies show that exclusive breastfeeding in the first few months, particularly for babies at risk, helps to decrease the risk or to delay the development of allergic symptoms.

If you suffer from allergies, it is best if the foods that cause a reaction are avoided during pregnancy and breastfeeding. However, the concept of babies being unsettled because of a reaction to something the mother ate, while possible, is less common than most people think. You should always seek expert help, say from a dietitian, before you make any radical changes to your normal diet.

Weaning usually makes the baby's condition worse. Contrary to popular belief, soy-based or goats'-milk infant formulas do not necessarily protect against allergies. Protein in each of these is as foreign as cows'-milk protein and can also cause an antibody response.

If you need to prepare special food for your baby, this can cause extra work and cost. Ask for a referral to a specialist who can give you skilled advice. Sometimes the support of others who are going through the same thing can be reassuring.

CHAPTER FIFTEEN

# Food fights

- *Breast refusal in the early weeks*
- *Some of the reasons your older baby might refuse the breast*
- *Sucking problems, including tongue-tie*

*What if your baby refuses to suck and in fact seems to fight the breast every time you offer it?*

Photograph by Lesley O'Donnell

All the books tell you that babies love breastfeeding, that they instinctively 'root' for the breast and seek the nipple. So what if your baby refuses to suck and in fact seems to fight the breast every time you offer it? Or what if she just can't seem to suck properly?

## Breast refusal

Breast refusal can happen out of the blue or gradually creep up on you. Reasons for your baby refusing to breastfeed vary with her stage of development. She may suck for a few minutes, then break away with

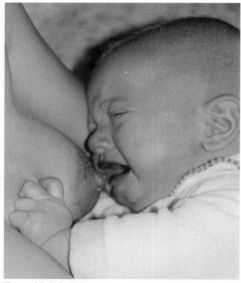

signs of distress and may refuse to continue. She may refuse to even begin sucking, although she is obviously hungry. Sometimes, your baby may not actually refuse to feed, but will be very fussy and difficult to feed. She may seem unwilling to start sucking or take a long time to get going. When she stops feeding, she may still seem restless and fidgety.

If your baby refuses to feed properly, you will naturally feel very distressed. You may already be feeling apprehensive, and perhaps not very confident, so when your baby turns away from your breast, you may misinterpret her behaviour and feel that she is rejecting you as a mother. In this situation, you may feel that you have no alternative other than to abandon breastfeeding. Fortunately, this isn't the case. Breast refusal is usually a temporary problem and there are strategies you can use to get past the problem.

*Photograph by Lesley McBurney*

### Some reasons for refusal in the early weeks

Sometimes a baby refuses to feed because she is tired, particularly straight after the birth if you have been given drugs during labour. She may like to just nuzzle and lick. Forcing her to the breast before she is ready will upset her (and you). Encourage her by expressing a little colostrum into her mouth. If she still refuses, don't worry, just tuck her in skin-to-skin with you and give her a little more time. She may show more interest when she is more alert.

Clothing around her neck and chin can also interfere with her natural 'rooting' reflex. When you touch her cheek, your newborn baby will automatically turn and lift her head towards that side. Holding her head or grabbing both cheeks will confuse her and may cause her to fuss, shake her head or appear to refuse the breast. A baby who is uncomfortable will not feed contentedly.

Breast refusal can occur if a baby is having difficulty attaching. This sometimes happens after the milk comes in and your breasts are very full. Try to express a little milk

*Photograph by Susan D'Arcy*

before you feed so that the areola is soft enough for your baby to latch onto.

It may also occur if your baby is having difficulty coordinating sucking, swallowing and breathing. If her nose is covered by her top lip or the breast, she will not be able to breathe. Nor is she likely to be attached to the breast properly. If your breast is very full, lift it up slightly with your free hand. If your breast is impairing her breathing, wrap her body closer in around your tummy, which should have the effect of bringing her nose away from the breast and her chin towards it. This is much more effective than pressing on your breast with your finger to create an air passage.

If your newborn baby has received bottles, she may already be used to the different sucking action required by a bottle teat, and she may take a little time to make the adjustment. It will be quicker and easier if she has no more bottles.

A sudden gushing flow of milk when it lets down can make your baby gag and become frightened. Express a little before the feed until the flow settles down. If she pulls away during a feed because of fast flow, let the flow subside before starting again.

## Some reasons for later refusal

○ A baby who has struggled to cope with a very fast flow in the early months, and has never enjoyed feeds, may begin to refuse at about three to four months when he has more control of his own movements.

○ If your baby has been used to milk just pouring into his mouth, he may not have learned to milk the breast efficiently, so that when your supply settles down and he needs to actually have to milk the breast, he may initially be fussy and irritable until his technique improves.

○ He may be frustrated if his appetite cannot be satisfied with the milk available, and is showing this frustration by refusing to feed.

○ If your let-down reflex takes longer than before to get going, your baby may become impatient. Try to trigger the let-down reflex before a feed by gentle massage or expressing, so that he is rewarded as soon as he comes to the breast. Consciously try to relax and use the suggestions elsewhere in this book to help trigger your let-down.

○ Your baby may also fight the breast if he is overtired or over-stimulated after a lot of handling and be too agitated or tense to feed. Try to make his day as low-key as possible until the problem resolves. Between feeds, cuddle him against your bare breast without offering it to him, to help him positively associate breast contact with comfort as well as food.

○ A blocked nose may make it difficult to breathe and feed and so he may refuse.

○ A baby with gastric reflux may be fussy when laid down flat to feed. Ask your medical adviser to check your baby.

○ Teething discomfort can also cause your baby to refuse to feed and may occur weeks before a tooth appears.

*Photograph by Susan D'Arcy*

○ Between the ages of four and six months, babies are very easily distracted. Feeding in a quiet room may help.

○ When your baby starts on other foods or drinks, he may refuse the breast if he has had bottles or cups of infant formula, boiled water or fruit juice. His appetite for your milk will be diminished, and your supply will drop. Your baby may also have become used to the different sucking action of the bottle. Unless you are actively moving towards weaning, try extra breastfeeds rather than bottle-feeds.

### refusing one breast

Babies sometimes just refuse one breast. If your baby has fallen asleep after one breast, he may have had enough. Many babies favour one breast over the other, usually because the milk flows more freely from that breast, but occasionally because they just have a preference for lying on one side. You may need extra patience to encourage him to take the less-preferred breast.

If he has a sore leg or arm after immunisation, he may suddenly refuse to feed on one side because he is lying on a sore spot. Try changing his position. If he has an ear infection, he may also refuse the breast, as lying down exacerbates the pain.

If your newborn consistently has problems feeding from a particular breast, or lying on one side, and you have ruled out the causes already mentioned, you might like to have him checked by a physiotherapist, or a paediatric chiropractor or osteopath. Sometimes babies are stiff on one side from their position in the womb, or from events during the birth.

## 'Am I the problem?'

There are a number of mother-centred factors that may come into play in breast refusal.

○ A sudden change in your diet can affect the taste of your milk and the smell of your body, causing your baby to refuse to feed.

○ A new perfume, spray deodorants that have strayed to your nipple, strong detergents that affect the smell of your bra, chlorine from a pool, or salt from the ocean, even smells from a trip to the hairdresser, can all possibly cause your baby to refuse. A quick shower will usually solve this problem.

○ Are you menstruating or ovulating? Hormonal changes can temporarily affect the taste of your milk. For some women, their baby fussing at the breast is an early warning that their period is due. Pregnancy can also cause a drop in the milk supply or a change in the taste.

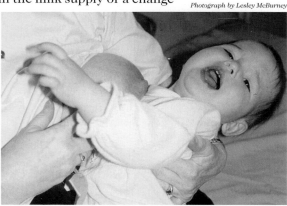

*Photograph by Lesley McBurney*

○ Some hormonal contraceptives have an effect on the taste of breastmilk. Make sure your doctor is aware that you are breastfeeding before a hormonal contraceptive is prescribed. Even some contraceptives which are routinely used in breastfeeding women can affect some babies' feeding behaviour. If you feel that this might be the problem but prefer to continue with this method of contraception, you may need to offer more frequent feeds until your baby gets used to the change in taste, or consider an alternative method of contraception, at least for a while.

## Changing needs

Finally, perhaps your baby is just not hungry. Feeding patterns do change. A previously enthusiastic feeder may start to be more interested in his surroundings than your breast. Most babies have longer breaks between feeds as they grow older. If there is no apparent reason for your baby refusing to breastfeed — you have eliminated all the usual breastfeeding management problems and your baby is well — it might mean that he is heading towards weaning.

This may come as a shock if you had planned to wean him slowly much later. You may feel very disappointed and take a while to accept that your baby no longer wants to breastfeed. Of course this does not mean that your baby no longer wants you. He will still want and need those special moments that you enjoyed together while breastfeeding, including lots of cuddles and reassurance when he is tired, sleepy or sick. If your baby weans suddenly you will need to express some milk occasionally to ensure that your breasts do not become overfull and uncomfortable.

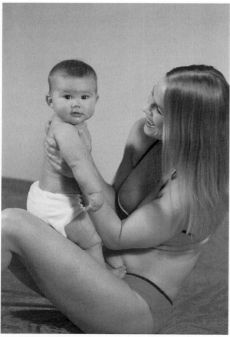

*Photograph by Dez Murad*

## Some suggestions for overcoming breast refusal

❍ Check that your baby is comfortable and correctly positioned and attached.

❍ Make sure that you are comfortable and relaxed yourself. Before feeding, practise the relaxation techniques you may have learned at antenatal classes.

❍ Offer the breast as soon as your baby begins to wake, or even while she is still asleep. She will usually respond better if she is not upset or crying. Change her nappy after the feed or before the second breast. Usually, the least likely time she will feed is just before a sleep.

❍ If necessary, help your baby take the breast into her mouth. If you have large nipples, try to shape the breast between your thumb and fingers so that it is easier for her to grasp. If your nipples are very small, try to pull them out gently just before you offer the breast.

○ Express your milk until it begins to flow easily so that your baby will be rewarded with milk as soon as she starts to suck.

○ Express a little milk on the nipple to encourage her to begin feeding.

○ Spend time skin-to-skin, carrying or cuddling your baby, without the expectation of her feeding, so that she can enjoy the closeness, but have the breast accessible should she want it.

○ Many babies relax and feed well if you feed them while taking a warm bath together.

## Sucking difficulties

In most babies, the sucking reflex is instinctive. However, a small proportion may need help to learn to suck effectively. This is more common in premature babies, those born before 34 weeks gestation when the suck-swallow instinct is not well developed, or in babies who are ill.

Occasionally, babies have sucking problems because of poor reflexes, or because they have poor mouth closure, or are affected by medication given to their mothers during labour or because they have suffered some sort of birth trauma.

### tongue-tie

Another cause of poor sucking is 'tongue-tie', where the tongue is anchored too tightly to the floor of the mouth so that it is not free or mobile enough for proper attachment to the breast. Babies' tongues are relatively shorter than the tongues of adults, but this doesn't impede sucking or speech development, as long as the baby can extend his tongue over his lower gum and it has sufficient mobility to form a trough under the breast tissue during feeding. By the end of their first year, most babies' tongues have grown so that they are fully mobile. True tongue-tie is fairly uncommon and tends to run in

*Young baby with a tongue-tie*

Photograph courtesy of
Dr Brian Palmer

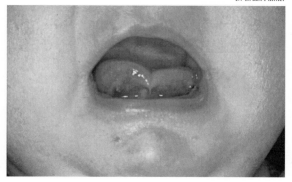

families, and seems to be more prevalent in certain populations. In some cases, where sucking problems relating to tongue-tie persist, snipping the frenulum can solve the problem.

However, most cases of poor sucking are caused by interference in the natural process of birth and establishment of breastfeeding (that is giving bottle-feeds or dummies), separating mother and baby at birth (so that breastfeeding establishment is delayed), labour medication that interferes with the baby's ability to suck, or the inappropriate use of nipple shields.

### suck training

Sucking problems can ultimately result in slow weight gains and failure to thrive in a baby, as well as nipple problems, mastitis and low milk supply in a mother. Patience and attention to correct positioning and attachment will usually overcome them. In some situations, a baby can benefit from special 'suck training'. This training should be provided by a lactation consultant, speech pathologist or occupational therapist with relevant skills and experience, who will usually work with you and your baby and teach you the techniques so that the three of you can work together as a team to overcome the problem.

CHAPTER SIXTEEN

# Providing expressed breastmilk for your baby

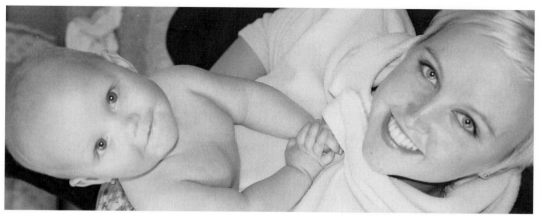

Photograph by Sarah McKay

*While the best way to remove milk from your breasts is undoubtedly by breastfeeding your baby, there may be situations in which this is not possible.*

- Mimicking a breastfeed and getting your let-down reflex to work
- How to hand expresss
- The different types of breast pumps
- How much to express
- Handling your expressed breastmilk and equipment

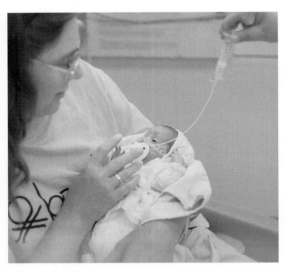

*Tube-feeding expressed breastmilk to a premature baby*

While the best way to remove milk from your breasts is undoubtedly by breastfeeding your baby, there may be situations in which this is not possible and you need to express your milk. Some of the reasons you may need to express could include:

○ Your baby was born prematurely or your baby is unable to suck effectively.
○ Your baby is hospitalised and you cannot be there for every feed.
○ You need to be hospitalised and your baby cannot be there for every feed.
○ You wish to go out and leave your baby with a caregiver.
○ You have to return to the paid work force, study or other commitments.
○ Your breasts have become very engorged and you need to express for comfort.

Some mothers like to keep a small store of breastmilk in the freezer to cater for unplanned situations in which they might have to be separated from their babies.

## Mimicking a breastfeed

When you express you are trying to mimic a breastfeed — the triggering of the let-down reflex; the pressure on the ducts in the breast just behind the nipple under the areola to start the flow of milk; and the rhythmic action of a baby's tongue and jaws to drain the available milk from the breast. You might find the mechanics of expressing a little awkward at first, but with practice you will get better at it.

The effective removal of milk from the breast is dependent on the let-down reflex. While the let-down reflex is a conditioned response to your baby's sucking, it can be encouraged by the sight or sound of your baby, or even just by thinking of him. It can also be triggered by stimulating the breast and nipple area with your fingers. The let-down reflex occurs several times during a feed or expressing session, and while you may only notice the first one, the subsequent let-downs may be stimulated by changing breasts as the flow slows during expressing.

## Triggering your let-down reflex

You can encourage your milk to let down when you are expressing:

*consciously try to relax*

If possible, try to express in a quiet, comfortable area, away from distractions. While expressing breathe slowly and deeply. Some mothers like to have a warm drink first or listen to soft music. Warmth (expressing after a warm shower, or warm face washers on the breast for a few minutes before starting) may also help. Expressing while sitting in the chair you use to breastfeed may help trigger your conditioned response.

*gently massage your breasts*

Stroke your breast towards the nipple with the flat of your hand or edge of a finger and gently roll the nipples between your fingers. While this will not actually push the milk out of your breasts, it can help trigger the let-down reflex.

*think about your baby*

Thinking about your baby will encourage your let-down reflex. If you are expressing because he is premature or sick in hospital, you might find it easier to express while you are there close to him, or just after you leave him. While you are away from him you might find even just looking at a photo of him will help your milk let down.

*have someone to support you*

Many mothers find expressing easier when they have an encouraging partner or friend there to support them. They may also give you a back and shoulder massage to help relax you. On the other hand, other mothers prefer to express in private because they feel under pressure if anyone is watching them.

A few mothers find it difficult to express, although they have a good milk supply and their babies are thriving. It is important not to judge overall milk production by the amount of milk that can be expressed. Especially in the period just after birth, amounts expressed are sometimes thought to be a guide to actual production. This is not so. Expressing might not be easy when you first try it — you might feel quite discouraged if, after all your efforts, you only manage a few millilitres or even a few drops! Take heart, gradually you will become more familiar with the feel of your breasts and how to make your milk flow more easily. When you are able to put your baby to the breast, you will find your supply will quickly increase to meet his needs.

## Cleanliness is important

When providing expressed breastmilk (EBM) for your baby, cleanliness is important so that the milk doesn't become contaminated during the process. This is particularly important if the milk is to be used for a premature or sick baby. In these circumstances, you should use the information in this chapter in conjunction with that of your baby's medical advisers, who may have additional requirements.

To ensure that your EBM remains germ-free:

○ You must thoroughly clean all containers used.
○ Before expressing, wash your hands thoroughly with soap and water, and dry them on new paper towel or a clean, unused towel.
○ Express directly into a clean container.
○ If you are storing your EBM in the same container that you are using to express into, as soon as you have finished, cover with a lid, label with the date and place it in the refrigerator. Otherwise, pour the milk into another clean container straight away before covering with a lid, labelling and refrigerating.

Note that, where EBM is to be used within six to eight hours, and the room temperature is lower than 26°C, and where refrigeration is not available, it is safe to leave the covered container of EBM out on the bench.

## How to hand express

Hand expressing is nearly always the gentlest way to express, even though some women take a little time to master the technique. With practice, hand expressing becomes quick and effective.

Any wide-mouthed container can be used to express into, or you

*Photograph courtesy of Dr Jane Morton*

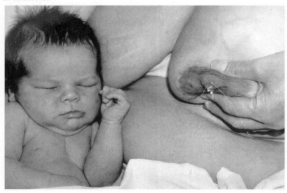

might prefer to use a specially-designed milk-expression funnel. Before you begin expressing, wash your hands and dry them with a clean towel. You might like to place a clean towel on your knees to catch any drips and to dry your hands if they become wet or slippery from your milk.

If you have the opportunity, having someone show you how to hand express is best, but if this is not possible, the photos on the next page show the basic technique step-by-step.

1. **Place your thumb and forefinger on either side of your areola,** well back from the nipple, with an imaginary line between them running through your nipple. A mirror might be of assistance while you are still learning if you can't see the lower part of your breast easily.

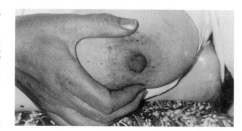

2. **Gently press your thumb and forefinger back into your breast tissue,** until you feel the bulk of the breast. If your breasts are full, your breast tissue might feel hard, lumpy or even a little sore. Treat your breasts gently; expressing should not hurt. When the let-down reflex occurs and the milk flows, the breast tissue softens and expressing becomes easier.

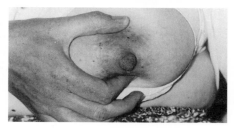

3. **Press your thumb and forefinger towards each other,** using a slight rolling action. This will compress the large ducts in the breast just behind the nipple and cause the milk to flow. Until the let-down reflex occurs, the milk may drip from the nipple and you might need to hold your bowl close to catch it. The let-down reflex may take several minutes — don't worry, the let-down is a conditioned response and will soon occur quickly each time you express.

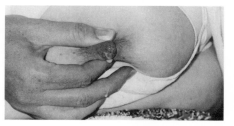

4. **Continue this compressing motion, in a rhythmical way,** until the let-down reflex is triggered. The milk can seem to spray from the nipple. Several jets of milk can occur with each compression.

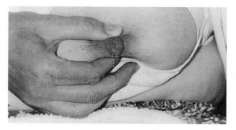

5. **When the flow eases, move to another section of breast,** working your way around the areola. Remember to place your finger and thumb on either side of the nipple, as before. If your hand tires, you might like to use your other hand.

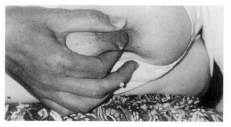

*Photographs by Yvette O'Dowd*

If the flow seems to decrease, try expressing the other breast in the same way. Change hands and breasts frequently if your fingers tire. You will find they become stronger with practice. You can swap between breasts until the milk no longer flows well.

When you are expressing to meet all your baby's needs, you should aim to have some longer and some shorter expressing sessions. During the longer sessions you might find you will get two or more let-downs and thus optimise milk production.

Some mothers use their right hand for their left breast and vice versa, others use the left hand for the left breast and their right hand for their right breast, still others use a combination. With practice you will find what is easiest for you. To avoid strain in your forearms and shoulders, relax and change your expressing positions frequently.

## Breast pumps

While a breast pump is not an essential part of everyone's breastfeeding experience, there may be times when a breast pump is a practical aid in continuing to provide breastmilk for babies who are regularly separated from their mothers. There are two main types of breast pumps available to suit a variety of situations.

*Piston-type pump with pull action*

Photograph by Yvette O'Dowd

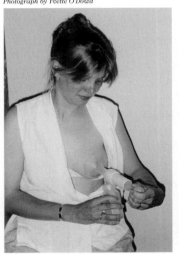

### Hand pumps

Manual or hand pumps are compact, inexpensive and portable. They come apart easily for cleaning and are designed for quick and easy use. Hand pumps are available from the Australian Breastfeeding Association and from many pharmacies. With new models coming onto the market all the time, you might like to ask for some advice before you buy. Most breast pumps have been tested by the Australian Breastfeeding Association and you can check with a breastfeeding counsellor if you are unsure about what type to buy.

#### piston-type pump

This pump has a cylinder that is angled downwards. A piston is pulled downward (on the first stroke) giving you good control of the suction pressure. The milk is collected in a small plastic feeding bottle that is fitted to the pump and most will accept standard feeding bottles. There are several variations on this type of pump, some with the piston action being created by squeezing a lever. Designs that allow your whole hand to work the piston (by pulling or squeezing) rather than just a finger or thumb, tend to be more comfortable to use over a prolonged period.

### cylinder pump

In this older style of pump (not so commonly used now), both cylinders and the pumping action are in a direct line. Relatively easy to use, you have direct control of the suction pressure. It is made of plastic, with the milk collected in the lower cylinder, which can then be used as a feeding bottle.

### pumps with rubber bulbs

Pumps with rubber bulbs, like the old 'bicycle horn pump' are not recommended. They can cause nipple damage and pain. The suction pressure is very difficult to gauge or control. They are also difficult to clean effectively.

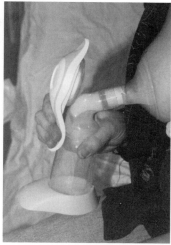

*Photograph by Yvette O'Dowd*

*Piston-type pump
with squeeze action*

## Electric pumps

There are two types of electric breast pumps — the compact, smaller pumps, some of which can be used with either batteries or mains power, designed principally for the use of one mother, and the larger electric pumps, the types most commonly available for hire and where each mother has her own milk collection kit. Some pumps can express both breasts at one time; some can convert to a hand pump for convenience. Most pumps are easily used on one breast, while your baby feeds on the other, allowing you to take full advantage of the let-down.

As the range of pumps currently available is quite wide, a breastfeeding counsellor will be able to help you in choosing the type most suited to your needs. Electric breast pumps can be purchased or hired from the Australian Breastfeeding Association or from pharmacies and possibly your hospital if you have been recently discharged. When the association hires an electric breast pump, each mother is shown how to use it correctly and is offered ongoing support from a trained

*Cylinder pump*

*Photograph by Yvette O'Dowd*

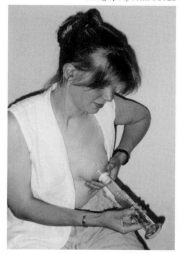

*Photograph by Yvette O'Dowd*

*Electric breast pump*

breastfeeding counsellor.

Even if you plan to use an electric pump, it is still worth learning about hand expressing and manual-pump expressing. Hand expressing is particularly useful to help your let-down before using the electric pump, and some mothers find they can get more out at the end of an expressing session, by finishing with hand expressing.

Some electric breast pump kits can be used as hand pumps, at times when you are unable to use the electric pump, or after you have returned the electric pump to the hiring agent.

## How much to express

How much you express depends on your reason for expressing. If it is just to reduce engorgement when you have too much milk you need only express enough to feel comfortable. This can be done by hand expressing in a warm bath or shower, unless you are planning to store your milk. If you have a blocked duct or mastitis, allow baby to feed as frequently as possible and express as much as you can after a feed.

### how much ebm will be needed?

It is very difficult to estimate the exact amount required by a baby for each feed, as babies vary widely in how much they normally take from the breast. If you are expressing for a baby who is premature or otherwise sick in hospital, the staff are likely to advise you about amounts that they wish to feed to your baby. You will be encouraged to build up your supply to what it would be if your baby was full-term.

Research has shown that the milk intake of exclusively-breastfed babies between one and six months is fairly constant for the individual baby but varies greatly between babies, with a range of about 500–1000 ml per 24 hours (with some being even higher or lower). The average is about 750–800 ml. In general, the late morning and afternoon feeds may be slightly larger than other feeds.

To roughly estimate how much is needed for a single feed, divide the estimated total amount by the number of feeds your baby normally takes in 24 hours. For example, if you assume 800 ml as the total, and your baby has eight feeds in 24 hours, then the average single feed volume will be 100 ml. You might like to make the late morning and afternoon feeds slightly higher and the other feeds a bit lower. Obviously, this is a very rough estimation, as not only are you unlikely to know exactly how much your baby takes over 24 hours, but the volume of milk taken at each feed also varies quite widely for most babies, and is dependent on a baby's appetite.

As a general rule, it is a good idea to express as much as you can, and store it in several small volumes, eg 50 ml each. In this way, baby can be offered a small feed and if she wants more than this, it is easy to take another 50 ml from storage and feed her that. This ensures your precious EBM is not wasted. If you are expressing on a regular basis, you will probably learn the approximate amount your baby likes to have at a feed, and you can use that knowledge to adjust the storage amounts.

If you are planning to express milk for just one feed to be given to your baby during your absence, you might either express a small amount (say 20–30 ml) at each feed during the preceding 24 hours, and keep this in the refrigerator, or express whenever it suits you sometime beforehand, and freeze the milk. Expressed milk should be cooled in the refrigerator before being added to already chilled or frozen EBM.

Depending on your baby's temperament, you can express before, during, after or between feeds, whatever you find easiest. Some mothers express one breast at each of the first two feeds of the day, then let the baby have extra sucking time at the other breast.

When you are away from your baby for a prolonged length of time, you might need to express a full feed or just enough for comfort. Some mothers overlook this when planning to be away from their baby for the first time, being so concerned about their baby's needs, they overlook their own! Don't forget to wear suitable clothing, take along tissues or a small towel if hand expressing, or a hand pump and perhaps extra nursing pads if you need them. Breasts that become overfull can be uncomfortable and may become engorged. A few minutes spent expressing while away from your baby can be well worth the effort.

## Suitable containers for storage of breastmilk

### plastic bags

Small sterile bags specially designed for storing breastmilk are available from the Australian Breastfeeding Association and from pharmacies.

These are made from plastics that do not leach into the milk, and they are thick enough to allow for long-term storage in the freezer. They also have the advantage that expressed breastmilk stored in these bags thaws more quickly than that stored in most other containers.

Photograph by Edwina Colvin

### baby feeding bottles

Glass is good for storage, the disadvantage being that it is more breakable than plastic. Important components of breastmilk such as antibodies and proteins do not adhere to glass as previously thought and glass is cleaned more easily. Hard plastic can be scratched, which makes thorough cleaning more difficult. Soft plastic can be punctured. When expressing just for the occasional feed it doesn't greatly matter which you use.

### small glass baby food jars, and other suitable containers

It is preferable to use small containers, suitable for one feed, to avoid wastage. Some mothers use thoroughly cleaned, plastic ice-cube trays — but these need to be covered and sealed well.

If you are collecting milk for a premature or sick baby, it is important to check with the hospital about suitable containers — they may supply them. Ask your medical adviser about any extra steps they require in the handling or storing of your milk. While breastmilk is best supplied fresh daily, your milk will keep for three to five days in the fridge (at 4°C) without losing much of its protective or nutrient quality.

## Preparing containers and breast pump parts

With the exception of the pre-sterilised EBM bags, all containers and breast pump parts used to collect or store breastmilk will need to be carefully cleaned before each use. If your baby is sick, be guided by your baby's caregivers concerning the level of care needed for cleaning equipment. Also, if you and/or your baby have thrush or you have another type of infection on your nipples, you might be advised to follow cleaning of your equipment with some form of disinfection treatment. Discuss your individual situation with your medical adviser, child health nurse, lactation consultant or an Australian Breastfeeding Association counsellor.

If you are expressing several times a day for a healthy baby, your manual breast pump or milk collection kit should be well rinsed in cold water after each use to remove surface milk, and should be stored in a thoroughly cleaned, closed container. Alternatively, you may simply store the pump or kit unrinsed in a closed, clean container or plastic bag in the refrigerator. At least every 24 hours, while the equipment is in frequent use, or after each time if the pump is only being used occasionally, it should be thoroughly cleaned, as described below.

In areas where there are separate water supplies for drinking and washing purposes, use drinking water to wash and rinse the pump equipment.

## Thorough cleaning

Thorough cleaning is important to make sure you have completely removed any milk residue or other material from the equipment and storage containers.

1. Wash your hands thoroughly with soap and water. Dry them on something clean, such as new paper towel or a clean, unused cloth towel.
2. Separate all parts of the containers. All removable parts of breast pump components need to be separated to ensure thorough cleaning. Rinse everything in cold water.
3. Completely remove all traces of grease, milk and dirt with a small amount of dishwashing liquid and hot water. Use a brush kept especially for this purpose.
4. Rinse at least twice in hot water.
5. Drain bottles and containers upside-down on clean paper towel and cover with more paper towel while they air dry. Before putting away, ensure no water droplets remain in the containers or on other surfaces. If any water remains, use more new paper towel to dry them.
6. Store dry equipment in a new plastic bag, plastic wrap, more clean paper towel or clean covered container until next use.

## Freezing breastmilk

1. Label the container with the date so that you use the oldest milk first.
2. Place the container (with the lid on) in the coolest part of the refrigerator.
3. When cold, place in the coldest part of the freezer.
4. Chilled milk can be added to frozen or previously-chilled milk as long as the container is returned immediately to the freezer or refrigerator.

Frozen milk will expand in the container, so fill only to three quarters full otherwise the container may burst.

If you are storing a lot of EBM in your freezer, and you go away, you might like to arrange for someone to check the freezer daily. Otherwise your EBM can be lost in the event of a power cut or a freezer malfunction.

## Thawing and warming breastmilk

Expressed milk will separate into several layers — this is normal, just give the container a gentle shake. Milk freezes in layers, but is readily mixed once thawed.

Frozen milk may be thawed in the refrigerator over 24 hours, or warmed quickly, but not in boiling water. Place the container under running cold water, and then gradually increase the water temperature until the milk becomes liquid. Do not leave it to stand at room temperature.

Warm chilled or thawed breastmilk in a jug or saucepan of hot water or in an electric drink heater, until the milk reaches body temperature. Test the temperature by dropping a little on to your wrist. Some mothers and babies are happy to use the milk thawed but not warmed.

A microwave oven should not be used to thaw or heat milk as it heats unevenly and may burn your baby's mouth. Research also suggests that microwaving changes the immunological and nutrient qualities of breastmilk. It is not necessary to boil your expressed breastmilk.

Very occasionally, some mothers find that their milk smells and tastes 'off' after storage in the refrigerator or freezer. This is not an indication that the milk is contaminated. This is thought to be caused by the action of digestive enzymes that are in the breastmilk, specifically those that break down the fats in the milk. Unfortunately, there is nothing you can do to remove this taste once it has developed, although the milk is quite safe to feed to your baby, as long she doesn't reject it due to the taste.

## Storage of breastmilk for home use

| Breastmilk status | Room temperature | Refrigerator | Freezer |
|---|---|---|---|
| Freshly expressed into container | 6–8 hours (26°C or lower)<br><br>If refrigeration is available, store milk there | 3–5 days (4°C or lower)<br><br>Store in back, where it is coldest | 2 weeks in freezer compartment inside refrigerator<br><br>3 months in freezer section of refrigerator with separate door<br><br>6–12 months in deep freeze (-18°C or lower) |
| Previously frozen — thawed in refrigerator but not warmed | 4 hours or less — that is the next feeding | 24 hours | Do not refreeze |
| Thawed outside refrigerator in warm water | For completion of feeding | 4 hours or until next feeding | Do not refreeze |
| Infant has begun feeding | Only for completion of feeding | Discard | Discard |

(Reproduced with permission from National Health and Medical Research Council 2003, Dietary Guidelines for Children and Adolescents in Australia Incorporating the Infant Feeding Guidelines for Health Workers. AGPS, Canberra. p 381.)

If this is a regular occurrence, one way to avoid it happening in future is to scald the breastmilk straight after expressing and before storage, to inactivate the enzymes. To do this, heat the breastmilk to just below boiling point and then cool rapidly, by placing the container in a bowl of ice. This only destroys a small portion of the anti-infective properties of the milk, and is a better option than to have to discard the milk if it develops the 'off' taste.

## Transporting expressed breastmilk

In some situations, expressed breastmilk needs to be transported — between home and hospital; work and home; home and the caregiver's. This can safely be done by collecting the milk in a clean container, storing it in the fridge and then transporting it in an insulated container with a freezer pack or crushed ice inside. Small bottles will even fit inside a wide-mouthed vacuum flask, with ice added to keep it cool. If the milk is frozen and it thaws during transportation, it must be used within 24 hours. Do not refreeze the milk.

## Feeding EBM to your baby

The method you choose to feed your baby EBM will depend on her age and preferences. You can use a small cup or a standard baby bottle. The benefits of using a small cup (or a special bottle with a cup attachment in place of the teat) are two-fold. A breastfed baby will usually accept a cup more readily than a teat and bottle if she is unfamiliar with them. A cup prevents any confusion between teat and breast. However, a baby having regular feeds of EBM, perhaps when her mother returns to the paid work force, may enjoy the sucking a bottle allows. If you wish to introduce a bottle and teat, don't begin until your baby has learnt to suck correctly at the breast and is gaining weight well. Some older babies may only accept a bottle from a person other than their mother. An older baby who refuses a bottle may take the milk more happily from a cup.

*Photograph by Lesley McBurney*

In some special situations such as if your baby is premature or ill, you might like to try a nursing supplementer, which delivers the milk to a baby through a fine tube, while she sucks at the breast. (See page 117.) Contact an Australian Breastfeeding Association counsellor for details of its use and suitability for your situation.

Regardless of whether you use a bottle or a cup, any left-over milk must be discarded at the end of a feed. The bacteria from baby's mouth will have contaminated the breastmilk and it should never be added to any existing supply of stored milk.

## Pacing bottle-feeds

Breastfed babies are used to being able to control the flow of milk as they feed and may find bottle-feeding from a fast-flowing teat quite stressful. It may appear that the baby is very hungry and gulping down the milk when in fact she might be doing all she can to swallow fast enough not to choke. One way to avoid this is to pace the feeds.

Advantages of giving babies control of the pace of feeds:
- It allows the baby to drink the amount she wants rather than the carer overfeeding her by effectively pouring the milk in.
- By not overfeeding a baby during the time she is away from her mother, it encourages her to breastfeed when mother and baby are together. This will help maintain the mother's milk supply.
- By avoiding overfeeding, the mother does not need to spend as much time expressing just to keep up with the amount of milk the baby is guzzling.

## How to pace feeds — instructions for carers

- Watch for hunger cues so that baby is fed when she is hungry rather than to a time schedule. Try to avoid using feeding to calm an unsettled baby as a first option. Perhaps there is another cause of unhappiness that could be resolved by cuddling, carrying or more attention. Obviously if these do not work, then a feed could be offered.
- Hold baby in an upright position, supporting the baby's head and neck with your hand rather than the crook of your arm.
- Use a slow-flow teat.
- Gently brush the teat down the middle of the baby's lips, particularly the bottom lip. This will encourage the baby to open her mouth wide, allowing you to pop the entire teat into her mouth, mimicking breastfeeding. Do not push the teat into the baby's mouth.

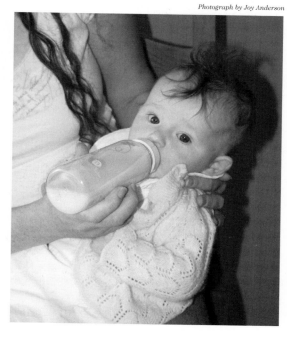

*Photograph by Joy Anderson*

- Tip the bottom of the bottle up just far enough that there is no air in the teat. As the feed progresses, you will need to allow the baby to gradually lean backwards, keeping the baby's head and neck in alignment, and the bottle will become almost vertical.
- Frequent pauses mimic a breastfeed and discourage the baby from guzzling the feed.
- Allow the baby to decide when to finish the feed rather than encouraging the baby to finish the bottle.

The Australian Breastfeeding Association produces the publication, *A Caregiver's Guide to the Breastfed Baby*, which is designed to be left with anyone feeding your baby in your absence. It contains detailed information on the thawing, warming and feeding of expressed breastmilk and the special needs of your breastfed baby. This is available as a photocopied sheet for a very nominal fee or free from the association's website. See: http://www.breastfeeding.asn.au/bfinfo/index.html

CHAPTER SEVENTEEN

# Working and breastfeeding

- Organising your return to paid work
- The logistics of working and breastfeeding, including expressing your breastmilk
- Childcare options
- Unpaid work

*You can maintain your supply of breastmilk while you juggle the conflicting demands of your paid work and family.*

Photograph by Prue Carr

There is no reason why you cannot continue to breastfeed your baby when you return to paid work. Breastfeeding your baby will not only be best for him, but best for your employer too. Everyone wins.

Babies who are not breastfed are more than twice as likely to be hospitalised in their first two years. Breastfeeding means fewer visits to the doctor and less time off work for you. It also saves you money. Breastfeeding your baby will also help you feel close and less anxious about separating from him. It will also give you an irreplaceable identity, letting him know that while he may have a loving caregiver, his mother has an irreplaceable role.

Increasingly, employers are implementing family-friendly work policies that help balance family and work. These policies are not just a public relations exercise to give the company a good image; they make sound economic sense. It doesn't matter if you are a salesperson, a tradesperson, or a professional, both you and your employer have probably invested quite a lot of time and money into your training, formal or informal, over the years.

*Photograph by Lesley McBurney*

Whether you are fortunate enough to be employed by a family-friendly workplace or not, it is vital that you talk to your employer about your plans to combine work and breastfeeding before you go on maternity leave. This will help you both plan for the future.

Find out your entitlements, either through the company's human resources section or through your union. Find out, too, whether the company provides any other benefits, not necessarily required by law, but which may have evolved through negotiations with other employees having babies. For example, a company may not have a written policy on working from home, but may have come to some agreement with another employee whose job allows such flexibility.

Think about how your paid job and your unpaid job of caring for your family may be better integrated to allow you to do both well, such as part-time work, or working from home for a while. While you may have more interruptions to your work day when you are breastfeeding and working at home, you will still be able to provide optimum nutrition for your baby while your caregiver attends to his other needs, and you will cut travel time and expense.

Talk to other employees with children about their experiences of returning to work and breastfeeding. Company policies may change as the needs of the workers change. A company which suddenly finds a large group of women taking maternity leave may decide to set up a special room for breastfeeding mothers to express and store their milk, if the employees point out that this will encourage mothers to return to work on schedule.

If your employer would like more information about working and breastfeeding, you could suggest that they contact the Australian Breastfeeding Association for information on the Breastfeeding Friendly Workplace Accreditation scheme.

## When to go back to work

Nobody knows how they are going to feel after the birth of a child, particularly a first child. Much depends on the type of birth you have, your age, the physical and emotional support you have, and of course, your own character and personality. Your return to work will also be influenced by the age and stage of your baby.

*Photograph by Chris Hoadley*

Returning to work before your baby is six weeks old will be extremely difficult. You may find you need at least this long to completely recover from the birth. New babies need very frequent feeding and not at regular intervals. It can take six weeks or more for breastfeeding to become well-established, with three months or even six months being much more realistic.

If you are lucky enough to have a choice, it is wiser not to make any firm commitments until your baby arrives. Try to make an arrangement that can be flexible. If you are entitled to take 12 months leave, ask your employer if you can take the full entitlement with the option of returning to work earlier, should you need or want to.

Everyone is different. Some women who, during pregnancy, could not imagine staying home with a small child, find that the rewards of their paid work are not as enticing as the rewards of mothering full-time, despite the economic disadvantage. Others who may have intended taking the full 12 months, find themselves climbing the walls after three months and aching for the intellectual and social stimulation of paid work. Others who believed that they were financially secure enough to take the full 12 months may suddenly find economic circumstances changed at home.

Whatever you decide, you can maintain your supply of breastmilk while you juggle the conflicting demands of your paid work and family.

## The logistics of working and breastfeeding

For most mothers, combining breastfeeding and paid work is a fast track to becoming an expert at expressing and storing breastmilk. It is useful to learn to express comfortably by hand, even if you invest in a breast pump to help you express more quickly and conveniently, or hire an electric pump from the Australian Breastfeeding Association or a pharmacy.

If you are only at work for a few hours, your baby may manage on only one feed while you are away, with some frozen expressed breastmilk as a backup, or some cooled, boiled water occasionally. If you work a full eight hours, your baby will need at least two or three feeds in this time. This will probably mean juggling your baby's own natural schedule to fit in with your work schedule. For example, if he usually feeds at around 5.30 am and 8.30 am, and you need to leave at 8.00 am for work, offer him a feed at 7.30 am instead.

If you express and freeze a supply of milk before you return to work,

*Photograph by Joy Anderson*

you will have your own personal milk bank and will not feel so concerned about running out.

Without you around constantly reminding him of his dinner, your baby's feeds may tend to be more regular and less frequent. His caregiver can keep him entertained and make sure that any unhappiness is really due to hunger. If your baby is unsettled because he misses the extra comfort of sucking, you may consider allowing him a dummy at unsettled times.

## Expressing your milk at work

If you cannot manage to feed your baby yourself during the day, you can still express your milk during your breaks and, providing that it is stored properly in clean containers at work, you can take it home with you to store. Your caregiver can give it to your baby while you are at work.

Workplace requirements for expressing and storing breastmilk are quite simple:

○ A private room (not the toilet area) with a comfortable chair.
○ A fridge to store expressed breastmilk (EBM).
○ A place to store your breast pump and other equipment.
○ Facilities to wash your hands and equipment.
○ Time set aside for expression of milk during the lunch break or other breaks if necessary. If extra time other than normal entitlements is needed, an agreement could be made that this time be made up in other ways.

Expressing may seem difficult at first, but most mothers in paid work say the benefits are worth the initial effort. You will probably find that you need to express your milk for your own physical comfort as well as to provide milk for your baby and to maintain your supply.

## Triggering the let-down reflex

Rushing out during your break to express milk for your baby while thinking about the work piling up on your desk and your boss anxious for your return, is not the best way of ensuring productive expressing. A good expressing technique is fundamental for getting the most milk, and triggering a let-down is part of this technique.

*Photograph by Lesley McBurney*

The let-down reflex is a hormonal response to your baby's sucking, but is also a psychological response, and it is this that you will need to trigger artificially when you are expressing milk. The best way to do this is to relax — easier said than done when you are in a different environment and have limited time. To help you relax, try a warm drink or snack, deep breathing exercises and even looking at a photograph of your baby. You may also use imagery. Think of milk flowing and a warm, pleasant place. Some mothers find it helps to take their mind and attention off how much milk is collecting in the bottle.

### Giving expressed breastmilk to your baby

You don't need to introduce your baby to a bottle just because you are returning to work. Expressed breastmilk may be fed to your baby in various ways, depending on his age and preferences. He may happily take your milk from a small cup or a bottle. If you do use a bottle, you do not need to introduce it until a few days before your separation. That's usually enough time for your baby to learn to cope with this new situation and is less likely to trigger problems such as breast refusal.

### Childcare options

No other subject seems to cause such polarisation among parents than the issue of child care. In most cultures, including our own, the ideal carer for an infant in its first 6 to 12 months of life is still considered to be his mother. But this does not mean that the mother must be the sole carer. Both babies and mothers can benefit from shared care.

Your choice in this matter will depend on your preferences and the age and personality of your baby, your type of work, the proximity of home and work and your budget.

*Photograph by Vicki Bell*

You may find that what suits you both at the start will change as your baby's needs change, so prepare to be flexible. You may end up combining various types of care. Make your choice according to the needs of your child and your own needs — not according to the views of others.

If you need to resume paid work within the first couple of months, the only arrangements likely to be compatible are work sessions that only last one or two hours, or those where you can work from home or take your baby with you. Your supply depends on the stimulation of your baby's sucking, so being there is important in the early days.

After their maternity leave expires, some women are lucky enough to have partners who are able to take extended leave or holidays or who have very flexible work arrangements that enable them to share the care of their baby.

If you cannot arrange care at home from a family member or nanny, work-based child care in an employer-provided crèche is ideal for the breastfeeding mother. Having baby close by means that you can feed him as he needs you. If work-based care is not available, and your baby is still very young, you may prefer the more intimate style of care offered by Family Day Care.

You may opt for a community or private child-care centre, where your baby will be looked after by a supervised team of carers. You could inquire about centres near your work so that you have the opportunity of going

*Photograph by Dianne Griffiths*

to the centre for scheduled feeds. A crèche close to your workplace will mean that your baby has to wait less time between feeds and you will be less stressed because you won't have to travel with a baby anxious for a feed.

### choosing a caregiver

Whatever childcare method you opt for, how do you choose a caregiver who is the right person for both your baby and you? It is important to ensure that your caregiver supports your decision to give your baby breastmilk. Don't be afraid to ask any potential caregivers about their attitudes to breastfeeding, and to change caregivers if you feel you are not being supported or you are even being undermined.

## Unpaid work

Despite the lack of economic reward, caring for a home and family is definitely work.

In the battle to recognise both the value of women's unpaid work, and the struggle women have to combine this unpaid work with their paid work, they can often find themselves fighting each other rather than the system.

The truth is that while 'women at home' and 'women at work' are often pitched against each other, statistics show that most women move in and out of these roles according to family circumstances.

The bottom line is that you make the best choice you can for your baby, your family and for yourself.

CHAPTER EIGHTEEN

# Growing up

- *How long to breastfeed*
- *Introducing solids*
- *All about weaning*
- *Some notes on relactation, biting and dental care in relation to breastfeeding*

*Breastfeeding is a precious gift that we, and only we, can provide as women for our young.*

Photograph by Dez Murad

The groundwork you put in to get breastfeeding off to a good start will mean that both you and your baby are reaping the rewards of your efforts. Breastfeeding a toddler is a joyous, and unforgettable, experience.

As the focus of community breastfeeding promotion has shifted to the importance of exclusive breastfeeding in the first six months, breastfeeding the older child has received less attention. However, the World Health Organization recommends six months of exclusive breastfeeding, then breastfeeding to at least two years and beyond in addition to appropriate complementary foods. Infant health authorities set no upper age limit to breastfeeding.

Studies over many years continue to show a 'dose-response' relationship between breastfeeding and a number of important health issues. That is breastfeeding for a short time is good; breastfeeding for a long time is better.

○ The immunologic components of breastmilk are maintained into the second year of lactation and are still providing protection for your toddler.

○ Weaned toddlers have more episodes of illness than those who are breastfed between the ages of 16 and 30 months.

*Photograph by Prue Carr*

○ Enhanced cognitive development has been shown to be positively associated with how long a child is breastfed (even after taking account of other influencing factors).

○ Breastfeeding for 12 months or more means your child is less likely to be overweight or obese later.

○ Breastfeeding for at least 12 months optimises long-term bone mineral density.

## Nature versus culture

All over the world, children were commonly breastfed for two to three years until the widespread introduction of Western artificial feeding products. Anthropologist, Katherine Dettwyler, has estimated that the natural weaning age starts at around two and half years when it is free of cultural beliefs. A key marker for weaning in other large mammals is a quadrupling of birthweight; this occurs around 27 months for male and 30 months for female children.

Australian breastfeeding data show that just over one in five infants are receiving breastmilk at 12 months. However, it's widely believed that breastfeeding into the second or third year is more widespread than these data suggest because many mothers don't admit to feeding their older children for fear of negative comments.

In our society, where mothers have an 'adult' life separate from their mothering responsibilities, or when they need or want to return to paid work, babies are usually pressured to separate from their mothers much earlier than they are developmentally ready.

Some people have a fear that continuing to breastfeed an older child will encourage over-dependency. In fact the opposite is true. Research shows that a secure attachment to their mothers through breastfeeding enables children to form attachments to others and to become more independent than a comparable group of bottle-fed children.

## Starting solids

If your baby is being breastfed according to need, your breastmilk will provide all he requires for at least the first six months of life.

You don't need to introduce any other food before this. In fact, if you do, your baby's appetite for breastmilk will be diminished, your supply will be affected and you may inadvertently begin the weaning process. Your milk contains the right amount of fluid, protein, fat, sugar, iron and other minerals and vitamins. A daily intake of just 500 ml can provide

*Photograph courtesy of Melanie Kilby*

about one-third of the protein and energy, 45 percent of vitamin A, and almost all of the vitamin C that a child needs in the second year of life.

Babies will not benefit from other foods until they are developmentally ready. Before about six months, babies have a natural tongue-thrust reflex that causes the tongue to push out a spoonful of food. By six months, they start to lose this reflex, making it easier for them to swallow solid food. A young baby's digestive system can't cope with the foreign fats and proteins that are found in other milks, eggs, meat, vegetables and cereals.

*Photograph by Barbara Glare*

Your baby has less chance of being allergic or intolerant to other foods if you wait until his system is ready for them. Often the push to start solids is to get a baby to sleep through the night, however it has been found that babies will not necessarily sleep any longer on solids than on an adequate feed of breastmilk.

At first your baby will only be interested in breastmilk, but gradually he will take an interest in what you are eating. At about the age of six months, he may even try to grab the food from your hand or your plate. This is part of the development process, rather than an indication that your baby is ready for solids.

You should always offer a breastfeed first. He will also be less hungry and irritable and more inclined to try the other foods that you are offering. If he is still having lots of breastfeeds (say six or seven), try just one meal of solid food a day, gradually building up to three. If you rush things, your milk supply will suffer and your baby will miss out on breastmilk, which is still the most vital food for his growth and development in the first year.

## Weaning

The sucking instinct is so strong in infants (and even in adults) that many children well past what is normally considered weaning age in our society, continue to suck dummies or thumbs and it is common to see a child of three or four still sucking a bottle. Is it any wonder, then, that many breastfed children cling to the comfort, warmth and reassurance of their mother's breast for a similar length of time? Be reassured that the time to wean is when you and your baby want to — not when others tell you to.

Weaning technically begins as soon as you introduce any food or fluid other than breastmilk. However, most people regard weaning as the process during which your baby has fewer and fewer breastfeeds until she is being completely nourished by other foods.

Ideally, you should follow your baby's lead. As children grow, so does their interest in the world beyond their mothers' breasts. Your baby's interaction with her new world, with new people and new foods and tastes, will encourage her to wean when she is ready.

There are many advantages of breastfeeding an older baby and weaning slowly. Your child will be able to outgrow infancy at her own pace and if she is ill and refusing to eat other foods you can be confident that breastmilk will provide valuable nutrients, protective factors and fluids. Your older child can also be weaned straight from your breast to a cup, thus avoiding the inconvenience of bottles. Many children who are weaned from the breast early develop a dependency on the bottle, from which they must be weaned later.

Ideally, weaning should be spread over several weeks or months, dropping one breastfeed at a time. Weaning is a process of letting go for both you and your baby, so it is important for the physical and emotional wellbeing of both of you that it occurs gradually and when you are ready.

*I don't feel like I want to wean him because it's the only time in the day that the world stops, once he starts feeding and I know that I'm going to sit or lie there till he's finished. It's just time when you're really alone together.*

*If I gave him a bottle and said here's a bottle, go and sit and drink it, it's not the same. The other really good thing is that when I'm feeding him I'm touching him and he's touching me. I just stroke him and cuddle him at the same time.*

## Baby-led weaning

You may be surprised to find that one day your baby makes it clear that he does not want to continue breastfeeding. He may fidget, refuse to feed or simply say that he has had enough. If this happens before the end of the first year or he is unwell, there may be other causes. However, if your toddler is healthy and has not shown interest in breastfeeding for a few days, he is probably ready to wean.

Many babies actually 'wean' their mothers by gradually refusing first one feed and then others over a period of weeks or months. Others wean themselves quite quickly. This can come as quite a shock — especially if you had planned a long and leisurely breastfeeding relationship. You may feel rejection and a general sense of loss. In this case, you may need help to accept your baby's decision. He will still need your closeness and will have had an excellent start to life.

Your milk supply may take some time to dwindle. Many women can express milk from their breasts for quite some time after their last breastfeed. You may need to express occasionally to keep your breasts comfortable and you should check regularly for lumps created by blocked ducts.

## Mother-led weaning

There are several reasons why you may want to wean your baby before he has shown that he is ready. You may be planning another pregnancy, or may already be pregnant. Many mothers continue to feed an older child throughout the pregnancy (and even go on to breastfeed both toddler and baby) and this is quite safe, but others prefer to wean. You may be returning to paid work and have chosen not to combine this with breastfeeding. You may have a medical condition for which you must take drugs that are contraindicated while breastfeeding. You may be bowing to pressure from friends or family to wean or you may simply have had enough. If you are no longer enjoying it and are feeling frustrated by your child's demands and he is healthy and happily eating other foods, this may be the time for some active discouragement.

### unweaning

Sometimes, circumstances such as illness or wrong advice can lead a mother to wean her baby unnecessarily and then regret it. You may have

*Photograph courtesy of Karleen Gribble*

been separated from your baby through illness, or your baby may have developed an allergy or illness after weaning and you may like to try to start breastfeeding again.

If you have adopted a baby, you may like to try to form a special bond with him by attempting to establish breastfeeding. Given sufficient stimulation, it is possible to induce lactation even when you have not given birth.

Whatever your circumstances, relactation or stimulating lactation if there has been no pregnancy, requires patience, determination, time, and above all, support. Contact the Australian Breastfeeding Association in your state; there are counsellors whose experience and knowledge in these areas will be of invaluable assistance.

## ouch! my baby has teeth

You may be advised by some well-meaning people that the eruption of your baby's first tooth is the signal to wean. While your baby may sometimes accidentally or playfully nip you before or after a feed, it is impossible for a properly-attached baby to bite, as his tongue is between the breast and his bottom teeth. Babies are generally adept at keeping their top teeth from clamping down, so there is no reason why you cannot continue to breastfeed your toothy baby. In fact, if his gums are sore or inflamed or itchy due to erupting teeth, he will probably be seeking the comfort of your breast more often.

Babies commonly get their first teeth between six and nine months of age — about the same time that they begin showing an interest in sampling other foods. Your milk will continue to provide valuable nutrients for the development of strong teeth and bones and will further protect your baby from illness during this sometimes unsettled and fussy time.

If your baby does try to give you a nip, after your first yelp, firmly and calmly tell him 'No' and remove him from the breast. He will soon learn not to bite the breast that feeds him. Biting usually only occurs when a baby is bored, distressed by teething, has discovered a new game, or to get your attention if your concentration is elsewhere.

A teething baby may try to bite anything handy to help relieve the pressure on his gums. To avoid further bites, encourage him to bite on something else hard for a few minutes before each feed or rub his gums with a special gel or something cool. These can be purchased after discussions with your pharmacist or medical adviser.

*Photograph courtesy of Charise D'Ath*

## dental care

While you may have read or heard that prolonged breastfeeding, especially at night, may contribute to dental caries, research shows that breastfeeding is actually protective against dental caries. Some children have vulnerable teeth for whatever reason and special care with their teeth is required. Some studies have shown a link between the dental status of mothers and their babies, so it is a good plan to visit your dentist to make sure your mouth is as healthy as possible. Sharing spoons or sucking on your baby's dummy to clean it can transfer caries-causing bacteria from your mouth to your baby's.

## How to wean

The process of weaning your baby can be as personal as deciding when to wean. Much will depend on your baby's personality, his need to suck and your circumstances. Here are some general guidelines, but overall it is best to play it by ear.

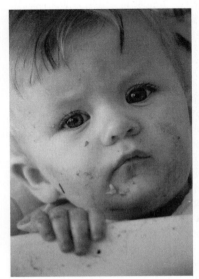

Whether you wean your baby onto a cup or a bottle will depend on his age. Start by not offering the breastfeed your baby seems least interested in, and then cut out one breastfeed every few days, or one each week (depending on your own comfort and your baby's willingness to cooperate) until you are only feeding once a day. Be prepared to breastfeed once every second or third day for a couple of weeks to keep your breasts comfortable. Alternatively, you may wish to hand express.

Offer a suitable family food instead of the deleted breastfeed. Breastfed babies are already accustomed, through your breastmilk, to the tastes of the foods you eat, so happily move to a wide range of taste sensations.

Your baby may need some extra cuddling time to help her through weaning, and some babies and toddlers especially need skin-to-skin contact at this time.

If your breasts are becoming lumpy and uncomfortable at any stage of the process, you can express a little or offer your breast to your baby briefly. Don't drain the breast

*Photograph by Mary van Luyn*

as this will only encourage more milk to be made.

If your baby seems unwilling to follow your lead, there are a number of things you could try:

○ Offer a dummy for extra sucking.
○ Give a substitute food before a breastfeed.
○ Offer only one breast at each feed and make sure she has plenty of other fluids.
○ Feed to a definite routine if this is possible.
○ Change daily routines to break the habit of feeding at particular times.
○ Encourage your partner or another family member to give substitute feeds at her usual breastfeeding times.
○ Encourage someone else to meet your baby's needs at night.

Mother-led weaning is a difficult balancing act that requires you to be firm and consistent but still loving. It's possible that your plan may backfire and your child may become more insecure and turn to the breast more. If she becomes ill or is distressed for any reason during the weaning process, it's best to back off for a while and start the process again when she feels better.

Weaning a reluctant toddler is sometimes a process of two steps forward and one step back, with several false stops along the way. However, as far as we know, most children start school weaned and toilet-trained despite their mothers' fears and frustrations.

*Photograph by
Shannon Bellette*

## If you need to wean quickly

If you need to wean quickly, say over several days, drop the alternate feeds in the first day, expressing just enough for comfort. You can cut out the rest of the feeds in the next few days, making sure that you still give your baby plenty of cuddles and attention.

The faster you wean, the more likely you are to experience a few days of painful engorgement. This will gradually subside, but initially you may need pain relief. Cold packs or chilled cabbage leaves applied to the breasts will also help reduce discomfort and swelling. Abrupt weaning also means that you are less likely to get back to close to your pre-pregnancy breast shape, and your hormones will be haywire for a while.

## Finding new ways to be close

Even if it was your decision to wean your baby, it can be an emotional time, especially if this is your last or only baby. While some mothers feel relieved to 'have their bodies back', others feel very sad that a special relationship has ended.

Hormones play a role in your mixed emotions at this time. After the weaning process, they will take a while to get back to normal. If they have not already done so, some women menstruate almost immediately, while others take a few months.

Whatever your feelings, you can be reassured that you have given your baby the best and that this is the beginning of another exciting stage in her life and yours.

*I remember feeling very sad that my son had chosen to wean. I felt great that he was ready, but I wasn't. I still get lots of lovely hugs though, where he will affectionately pat my breasts as though he's saying: 'I remember and thanks Mum.'*

## In conclusion

Breastfeeding is a remarkable experience. You have the satisfaction of knowing that you are giving your baby not only a healthy beginning, but also a lifetime advantage; you have the confidence that comes from appreciating that it is something that only you can do for your baby; you know that the intensity and the intimacy of breastfeeding creates a lifelong bond between you and your baby. That's what the Australian Breastfeeding Association wants for you and for all mothers.

*Breastfeeding is a precious gift that we, and only we, can provide as women for our young. Women have a right to breastfeed, to have faith in our own ability to succeed. We can do anything — we are certainly capable of this!*

*Photograph by Perfect Image Photography and courtesy of Belinda Morrissy*

CHAPTER NINETEEN

# The importance of sharing

- *How the Australian Breastfeeding Association began*
- *Counselling, shop-from-home and breast pump hire services*
- *How to contact the Australian Breastfeeding Association*

*The needs of all mothers and their babies are of vital importance. That's why the Australian Breastfeeding Association and its work is so important.*

Photograph by Prue Carr

Breastfeeding your baby is an exciting and rewarding experience for you both. However, as in all things that are worthwhile, there are usually both joys and difficulties. At both times, it helps if you are able to share your thoughts and feelings with like-minded people.

These may be your family, your friends, other mothers you met while you were pregnant or in hospital or through your child health nurse, at playgroup, the pool, the library, the playground, or by attending your local Australian Breastfeeding Association group.

When you first become pregnant, you will suddenly notice all the other pregnant women around you — and all the information targeted at them. You may be sitting in your doctor's waiting room, flicking through a magazine on parenting, and see an ad for the Australian Breastfeeding Association, or a poster on the wall, or a health department pamphlet about the importance of breastfeeding with the association's contact number.

Photograph by Natasha Paes, courtesy of Fairfax Community Newspapers

The needs of all mothers and their babies are of vital importance. That's why the Australian Breastfeeding Association and its work is so important — as a lobby group, to ensure that government policies reflect the needs of families; as an educator; and as a great support network for breastfeeding mothers and their families. The association informs them and supports them in their decision to feed their babies naturally and gives them the knowledge and confidence to do so successfully.

## How six women began a revolution

Mary Paton was a young mother in 1964 when she and five friends began the Nursing Mothers' Association, later called the Nursing Mothers' Association of Australia (NMAA) and now called the Australian Breastfeeding Association. Mary had trouble breastfeeding her first child, and was finding it difficult to find good breastfeeding information. The friends decided to form a self-help group for breastfeeding mothers.

Mary's home in Balwyn (in Melbourne) became the first unofficial headquarters for the association. Forty years later, the Australian Breastfeeding Association, with its head office in Melbourne, has approximately 10 000 subscribers, local groups in every state and is recognised both in Australia and overseas as the country's, and indeed one of the world's foremost authorities on breastfeeding. The Australian Government and health professionals agree that breastfeeding is essential for healthy babies and that breastmilk is a complete food that is all a baby requires in its first six months.

However, when Mary Paton and friends first met to form the association, breastfeeding was not considered cool. The 1960s were in full swing, rock 'n' roll had revolutionised the music industry and social mores were changing. Freedom was the catchcry of the era. Beehive hairstyles, miniskirts and stiletto heels were symbols of womanhood and the baby feeding bottle was a symbol of motherhood.

*Photograph by Prue Carr*

*Mary Paton today*

The more gentle revolution started by Mary Paton and friends is not as well documented, but its effects have been just as far-reaching, if not more so.

It wasn't that breastfeeding was actively discouraged at the time — it just wasn't encouraged. Mothers were given the choice of breastfeeding or bottle-feeding, but if complications arose, it was assumed that bottle-feeding was an equal substitute. In fact, as long as there was a bottle and a scientific infant formula around, persevering with breastfeeding was considered fanatical and risky.

The six foundation members soon found the fledgling association had outgrown the nest. When the space under the Paton marital bed could no longer hold its documents, it was decided that a proper office should be set up. This was achieved through selling memberships and designing, making and selling breastfeeding and mothering aids.

The association is one of the largest women's organisations in Australia and receives over 260 000 counselling contacts per year to its breastfeeding counsellors, many of which are via the free Breastfeeding Helplines in each state.

Over the last 40 years, more than 20 000 women have qualified as breastfeeding counsellors and benefited from the specialist skills they acquired through the association's highly-regarded volunteer training scheme.

In providing seven-day-a-week Breastfeeding Helplines, over 637 000 volunteer hours are given by counsellors each year — this represents a contribution equivalent to over ten million dollars.

The association's Lactation Resource Centre has one of the most comprehensive collections of breastfeeding information in the world, and provides a scientific basis for the association's information services and breastfeeding policies.

Involvement with the Australian Breastfeeding Association has also given many women not only the confidence to breastfeed, but the confidence to achieve in other areas too.

This book contains the combined wisdom of thousands of women — those who had the courage and conviction to have founded the association, its members and those health professionals who support its goals.

We hope that you will take this wisdom for yourself, make good use of it, enjoy it, and pass it on to your friends, your daughters, and their daughters. You may even have your own pearls to add to it as you learn what it is to be a mother in this changing world.

## About the Australian Breastfeeding Association

### Our Vision

For babies to breastfeed exclusively for six months, with ongoing breastfeeding for as long as mother and baby desire.

### Our Mission

As Australia's leading authority on breastfeeding, we educate and support mothers, using up-to-date research findings and the practical experiences of many women. We work to influence our society to acknowledge breastfeeding as the norm for infant nutrition.

### Our Aims

○ To provide factual information for all women to make informed choices about feeding their babies and their parenting styles.
○ To be active participants in government inquiries and committees concerning breastfeeding, and provide input into government policy development.

- To give women confidence in themselves as women and mothers, through skill acquisition, community networks and positive role models.
- To create an awareness in the community of the importance of human milk, breastfeeding and nurturing.
- To work with health professionals and others in the community to provide an optimum environment for women to establish and continue breastfeeding.

## Counselling service

Australian Breastfeeding Association counsellors help thousands of mothers every year. As breastfeeding mothers themselves, they know that breastfeeding does not always seem easy. Their experience can reassure new mothers and give them the knowledge to understand how breastfeeding works. Counselling is available to subscribers and non-subscribers alike.

*Photograph courtesy of Annette Wallace*

Breastfeeding counsellors are all trained volunteers. All have breastfed at least one baby for at least nine months and undertaken the association's breastfeeding counsellor training course to qualify. They provide counselling and breastfeeding information to any person seeking help. Counsellors continually update their breastfeeding knowledge and counselling skills. They are not medically trained and so cannot give medical advice. Their areas of expertise are breastfeeding management and mother-to-mother support.

## Code of ethics

The Australian Breastfeeding Association has a code of ethics, which is binding upon all its breastfeeding counsellors and other members who represent the association in any way.

Under the code of ethics, counselling is free to all. In cases where payment is made (eg lectures), any such payment is the property of the association. The association's meetings and mailing lists are not used to promote individuals or other organisations, nor to promote political, sectarian, racial or other causes.

A personal and friendly mother-to-mother approach is the very essence of the Australian Breastfeeding Association. Counsellors do not advise mothers, but offer suggestions on a mother-to-mother basis. They must not be dogmatic or fanatical. They refer the mother to her medical adviser or any other appropriate person when medical advice is required. Names and details of a mother who has received counselling are strictly confidential.

Counsellors deal cooperatively with doctors, hospitals and child health nurses. The discussion of particular doctors, hospitals, nurses or health centres, both at meetings and in conversations, is discouraged.

Help with breastfeeding is available by telephone, at group meetings or by email. The association's website (http://www.breastfeeding.asn.au) has full details of the email counselling service.

## Telephone counselling

All states have a Breastfeeding Helpline, with counsellors participating on a roster system. You can also look under Australian Breastfeeding Association in your local White Pages. (Some books may still have the association listed as Nursing Mothers' Association of Australia.) The Helplines are available seven days a week. Counsellors are answering calls in their own homes, so please take this into consideration when calling.

## Breastfeeding Helplines

| | |
|---|---|
| ACT/Southern New South Wales | (02) 6258 8928 |
| New South Wales | (02) 9639 8686 |
| Queensland | (07) 3844 8977 or (07) 3844 8166 |
| South Australia and Nothern Territory | (08) 8411 0050 |
| Tasmania | (03) 6223 2609 |
| Victoria | (03) 9885 0653 |
| Western Australia | (08) 9340 1200 |

## Mothers Direct shop-from-home service

The Australian Breastfeeding Association has its own shop-from-home service, Mothers Direct, which offers a range of quality products, many designed and made exclusively for the association. Products include a range of breastfeeding resources and parenting products. The Mothers Direct catalogue is online for you to view and select from. See: http://www.mothersdirect.com.au

## Electric breast pump hire

Electric breast pumps are available for hire from the Australian Breastfeeding Association. Pumps are available to mothers for short-term or long-term hire to enable them to express their milk for their babies. Each mother needs to purchase her own new personal milk collection kit to use with the hired pump.

Subscribers to the association receive a discount of 50 percent on pump hire charges. A fully-refundable deposit is also required at the time of hire.

Breast pumps can only be hired from a trained Australian Breastfeeding Association counsellor. The counsellor will be able to help the hirer with any questions about using the pump, expressing and storing breastmilk and all other aspects of breastfeeding.

### Contacting the Australian Breastfeeding Association

*Head office*

Street address:
   1818–1822 Malvern Road, East Malvern, Victoria 3145 Australia
Postal address:
   PO Box 4000, Glen Iris, Victoria 3146 Australia
Telephone:
   (03) 9885 0855 (from outside Australia +61 3 98850855)
Facsimile:
   (03) 9885 0866 (from outside Australia +61 3 98850866)
Email:
    info@breastfeeding.asn.au
Website:
   http://www.breastfeeding.asn.au

## Australian Breastfeeding Association booklets

The following publications are available from local Australian Breastfeeding Association groups or via mail order within Australia by phoning 1800 032 926, or via the Internet at: http://www.mothersdirect.com.au.

Booklets:
*Introduction to Breastfeeding*
*Breast and Nipple Care*
*Breastfeeding After a Caesarean Birth*
*Breastfeeding and Hospitalisation*
*Breastfeeding Babies with Clefts of the Lip and/or Palate*
*Breastfeeding Through Pregnancy and Beyond*
*Breastfeeding Triplets, Quads or More*
*Breastfeeding Twins*
*Breastfeeding, Women and Work*
*Breastfeeding Your Baby with Down Syndrome*
*Breastfeeding Your Premature Baby*
*Coping with Breast Refusal*
*Especially for Grandparents*
*Expressing and Storing Breastmilk*
*Gastro-oesophageal Reflux and the Breastfed Baby*
*Increasing Your Supply*
*Introducing Solids*
*Keeping Baby Cool*
*Looking After Yourself*
*Relactation and Adoptive Breastfeeding*
*Sex and the Breastfeeding Woman*
*Survival Plan*
*Too Much*
*Understanding Wakeful Babies*
*Weaning*
*Why Is My Baby Crying?*
*Your Toddler and the New Baby*

Leaflets:
*Caregiver's Guide to the Breastfed Baby*
*Lactation Suppression*

# FINALLY

*Jill Day*

This book is based on the practical experiences of thousands of mothers and firmly grounded in scientific fact. It is as simple, and as complex, as breastfeeding itself. We hope that we have given you what you need to support your commitment to breastfeeding your baby. If you haven't found the answers to all your questions, we encourage you to contact the Australian Breastfeeding Association. Its resources are far broader than it would ever be possible to include in one book.

This edition of *Breastfeeding ...naturally* would not have been possible without the dedication and skills of many remarkable women.

Thank you to the subscribers who shared their thoughts about their own breastfeeding experience as well as their precious photos.

Thank you to the many breastfeeding counsellors who helped in the development of the content and in bringing it to print.

Thank you to Jane Cafarella, the book's original editor for her contribution to this new edition, to Lesley Huxley who began the task of revising the text and to Heather Rutherford for compiling the comments.

Very special thanks to Kate Mortenson, the manager of the association's Lactation Resource Centre, for her skills in making sure our information was correct and for her unwavering commitment to making this new edition a reality.

A special thankyou too, to Joy Anderson, for expertise in both lactation information and in formatting and print production.

My personal thanks to my friends and colleagues in the Australian Breastfeeding Association who have supported and encouraged me, not only in the task of editing this book, but also in my ongoing commitment to breastfeeding over the years.

Love and thank you also to my three daughters for sharing me with the association and with this book and for reminding me just how important breastfeeding is to each of us.

**Jill Day**
**Editor 2006**

# ACKNOWLEDGMENTS FOR PICTORIAL CONTENT AND DESIGN

*Joy Anderson*

Sincere thanks to Nicole Patterson (cover designer) and Roxanne Iwinski (basic layout designer) for providing their time and considerable expertise free of charge to the Australian Breastfeeding Association.

Thanks also to the photographers for their generosity and to the families who have provided subjects for the photographs.

A special thankyou to Yvette O'Dowd for not only her photographic expertise, but also for her considerable efforts to make sure I had a large range of photographs available for incorporating into the layout of this book. Thanks also to Barb Glare for assistance with liaising with photographers and for obtaining photographs.

Last but not least, special thanks to my husband, Keith Anderson, for technical assistance with the publishing software, and for support and encouragement throughout the process of production.

**Joy Anderson**
**Designer/typesetter**

# INDEX